Praise for RECOMMENDED

I found the read to be both relevant and valuable on a personal and professional level. The book covers the referral strategy topic in an exhaustive and detailed manner.

The learnings from this book are practical and portable to all areas relating to the 'science' of engineering, executing and maintaining a referral strategy (both at a professional and personal level). I took away a mountain of 'pearls of wisdom', thank you.
COLIN WRIGHT
SENIOR VICE-PRESIDENT, GLOBAL SALES DEVELOPMENT, MASTERCARD

This book offers no-nonsense, straightforward and practical advice to any business which needs to boost its sales. Leads generated through referrals tend to be the most likely to convert to business, making this book an essential tool for any salesperson.
DR TONY ALESSANDRA
AUTHOR OF *COLLABORATIVE SELLING* AND *THE PLATINUM RULE*

This book shows you how to build a golden chain of referrals that enable you to sell more, faster and easier than ever before.
BRIAN TRACY
CO-AUTHOR OF *THE NEW YORK TIMES* BESTSELLER *NOW, BUILD A GREAT BUSINESS!*

Recommended is a practical guide that reinforces concepts that, if practised, will lead to a more focused approach in cultivating referrals. In my experience, strong referrals are more likely to convert to business than any other form of lead-generation. However, those referrals are rooted in strong relationships. Andy does a great job in dispelling the myth that salesmen need to pitch at every opportunity, instead emphasising the role of relationship building in strong referral generation.
ERICH GERTH
EXECUTIVE DIRECTOR, CEO GLOBAL BUSINESS DEVELOPMENT, AVIVA INVESTORS

A powerful network is essential for any successful business and Andy is the king of the networking scene. His new book is a must read if you are serious about building your tribe of followers and enjoying the rewards that network can then offer you.
RACHEL ELNAUGH
ENTREPRENEUR, BBC TV 'DRAGON' AND AWARD-WINNING BUSINESS MENTOR

In this book Andy Lopata demonstrates how so many businesses ignore potentially their most powerful resource – their networks. Andy's in-depth, practical advice will show you how to both build and profit from the relationships in your network.

IVAN MISNER
NEW YORK TIMES BESTSELLING AUTHOR AND FOUNDER OF BNI AND THE REFERRAL INSTITUTE

How to open the door in sales is the first step in the business-growth process. Andy Lopata addresses this fundamental challenge with focus on warm-lead generation through referral. Proven to be a more likely way to convert business, this book is an essential tool for any ambitious sales person or business owner.

LARA MORGAN
FOUNDER AND FORMER CEO, PACIFIC DIRECT GROUP AND FOUNDER OF WWW.COMPANYSHORTCUTS.COM

What's so good about this book is that it's based on Andy's own experience and practice. Powerful referrals are the foundation for any successful business and this is a practical guide to both receiving and giving high quality introductions. Everything that Andy has done for Big Issue Invest demonstrates that he really walks his talk.

NIGEL KERSHAW OBE
CEO, BIG ISSUE INVEST AND GROUP CHAIRMAN, THE BIG ISSUE COMPANY LTD

This book is both thought provoking and practical. The advice offered makes perfect sense and the reader is constantly shown how to apply it to their own business.

JOHN JANTSCH
AUTHOR OF *DUCT TAPE MARKETING* AND *THE REFERRAL ENGINE*

Andy Lopata is a great example of a champion. Through Andy, I have, over the past two years, picked up the phone and called potential sponsors, speakers, volunteers and partners, and the reason they answer my call is that my champion – Andy – has paved the way.

MICHELLE BRAILSFORD
TALENT MANAGEMENT, BBC WORLDWIDE AND CO-CHAIR, EUROPEAN PROFESSIONAL WOMEN'S NETWORK

Andy is a very experienced networker who has taken his own highly successful approach and translated it into an effective and practical guide.

KEITH FERRAZZI
BESTSELLING AUTHOR OF *NEVER EAT ALONE* AND *WHO'S GOT YOUR BACK*

Developing your network is a prerequisite of any successful businessperson. Whether for sales generation or your personal development, who you know is still as important as what you know. In this book, Andy delivers some tried-and-tested techniques that anyone can use to increase their sphere of influence and ultimately the profile of themselves as an individual or as a business. A must read.

PHIL JONES
UK SALES AND MARKETING DIRECTOR, BROTHER UK

A stimulating and interesting read. Strong, enduring, intimate relationships are critical to be successful in business – Andy is an industry expert in that regard and his book is rich in terms of hints, tips, strategies and wisdom to help you build and retain better relationships through effective networking.

PETER RYAN
CHIEF CLIENT OFFICER, LOGICA

Recommended

Recommended

HOW TO SELL THROUGH NETWORKING AND REFERRALS

Andy Lopata

**Financial Times
Prentice Hall
is an imprint of**

PEARSON

Harlow, England • London • New York • Boston • San Francisco • Toronto
Sydney • Tokyo • Singapore • Hong Kong • Seoul • Taipei • New Delhi
Cape Town • Madrid • Mexico City • Amsterdam • Munich • Paris • Milan

PEARSON EDUCATION LIMITED

EDINBURGH GATE

HARLOW CM20 2JE

TEL: +44 (0)1279 623623

FAX: +44 (0)1279 431059

WEBSITE: WWW.PEARSON.COM/UK

FIRST PUBLISHED IN GREAT BRITAIN IN 2011

ISBN: 978-0-273-75796-2

BRITISH LIBRARY CATALOGUING-IN-PUBLICATION DATA
A CATALOGUE RECORD FOR THIS BOOK IS AVAILABLE FROM THE BRITISH LIBRARY

LIBRARY OF CONGRESS CATALOGING-IN-PUBLICATION DATA
A CATALOG RECORD FOR THIS BOOK IS AVAILABLE FROM THE LIBRARY OF CONGRESS

THE PUBLISHER IS GRATEFUL TO THE NIELSEN COMPANY FOR PERMISSION TO REPRODUCE FIGURES
5.1 AND 5.2, TAKEN FROM THE JULY 2009 NIELSEN GLOBAL ONLINE CONSUMER SURVEY: TRUST, VALUE
AND ENGAGEMENT IN ADVERTISING.

10 9 8 7 6 5 4 3 2 1
15 14 13 12 11

DESIGNED BY DESIGN DELUXE
TYPESET IN 9.5 PT SWISS 721 BT LIGHT BY 30
PRINTED AND BOUND IN GREAT BRITAIN BY ASHFORD COLOUR PRESS LTD, GOSPORT, HAMPSHIRE

This book is dedicated to everyone who has supported, advised, referred and recommended me over the years.

Thank you for your support.

Contents

Acknowledgements xi

Preface xv

Introduction xix

PART 1 WHY YOU NEED TO GET RECOMMENDED 1

1 What is a referral? 3

2 The role of networking 15

3 Current approaches don't work 27

4 You can't just throw mud at a wall 37

PART 2 THE FOUNDATION OF THE ULTIMATE REFERRALS STRATEGY 55

5 The role of trust in a referrals strategy 57

6 Do people understand how to refer you? 79

7 Who has the best opportunity to refer you? 101

PART 3 HOW YOUR NETWORK CAN HELP YOU GENERATE REFERRALS 111

8 The six degrees of separation and how they influence your referrals strategy 113

9 Where will your referrals come from? 131

10 Referrals within an organisation 145

11 How to select the right networks for you 153

PART 4 HOW TO GET YOUR NETWORK TO REFER YOU 177

12 Inspiring people to refer you 179

13 When to ask for referrals 199

14 Referring others with confidence 205

PART 5 TOOLS YOU CAN USE 219

15 LinkedIn as a referral tool 221

16 The Referral Book 239

17 Results you can rely on 249

In a nutshell: Ten steps to an effective referrals
   strategy 259

Further resources 267

Index 271

Acknowledgements

You would be very disappointed, I'm sure, if a book on the power of referrals and networking was written without the help of a host of people from within the author's own network. Well, I would hate to disappoint you!

This book is being published by one of the largest business publishers in the UK, and carrying the imprint of one of the most respected business newspapers in the world, thanks, naturally, to a referral.

Bruce King, author of *How to Double Your Sales*, referred me to Liz Gooster at FT Prentice Hall. Bruce's introduction fulfilled all of the requirements of a good referral. He told Liz about me and why she should be interested in speaking with me, and he connected us so that I had permission to call and Liz was expecting my call.

Liz and I met a few days later and from there Liz worked tirelessly with me not only to get the book accepted by Pearson but also to make it as good as it could be. Thanks to Bruce and Liz for your help and support.

Many people ask me how I found the time to write a book, and it's certainly not a task you take lightly. This is, in fact, my third book but the first one I have authored on my own. I was never alone through the process though, thanks to the excellent guidance and support offered by my 'book midwife' Mindy Gibbins-Klein. Mindy offers a fantastic service to prospective authors, helping with the planning and guiding you through the process. This book might still be an idea in my mind without Mindy's support.

Speaking of the book being in my mind, the catalysts for making me take responsibility for getting my ideas published were Kate

Trafford and Tiffany Kay. Kate and Tiffany dragged me out of the audience at a showcase talk for Academy for Chief Executive Chairmen. During their session with me they encouraged me to commit to writing the book and set a deadline. Doing something like that in front of a large audience pretty much commits you to doing something about the goal. Kate and Tiffany are both now writing their own books, so what goes around comes around! Thank you both.

There is one common thread between my three books, other than me of course. Jo Parfitt is an excellent editor and did sterling work on *Recommended* before it went to Pearson. Once at Pearson I want to thank Emma Devlin for her help in bringing the book to life.

Thank you also to Rosie Slosek and Sarah Hilton for reading through drafts of the book at various stages of development and for giving me valuable and honest feedback.

I didn't want to have the arrogance just to share my own world view, instead believing that the thoughts and ideas of other people working in this, and related, fields would enhance the arguments made within the book. I have therefore turned to a number of people in my network, and outside, for their thoughts. I am very grateful for the time of many people, some of whom, alas, didn't make it into the final version.

Thanks to Australia's 'Trust Lady', Vanessa Hall, for giving me her time for an extensive interview. Thank you also to Mike Burnage, Andy Preston, Peter Thomson, Howard Nead, David Baum, Tim Farazmand, James A Ziegler, Angela Marshall, Lesley Everett, Warren Cass, William Buist, Neil Mutton, Martine Davies, Alan Stevens, Tony Westwood, Dave Clarke, Nancy Williams, Mike Southon, Daniel Priestley, Derek Bishop, Servane Mouazan, Aron Stevenson and Tim Bond for sharing their stories and their wisdom.

In Chapter 15, on using LinkedIn as a referral tool, we use the example of Mark S from Ford to show how a third degree connection can be found and made. Thanks to Mark Simpson for allowing us to use him as an example and to my first and second degree connections, Foluke Akinlose MBE and Nicole Yershon, for passing my message on to Mark. There ... it works!

Thanks also to Maggie Berry from Women in Technology for the use of her testimonial from LinkedIn.

I've had some great people offer endorsements for the book, to help convince you that it is worth exploring its pages. My thanks go to everyone who provided such an endorsement, along with the people who introduced me to some of them, in particular Ivan Misner, Vanessa Vallely, Rod Sloane and Jennifer Rademaker.

Thanks to Jason Sullock and his team at Sage for their support in promoting the book to customers of their ACT! database system. In the modern world, companies need to have more than a simple transactional relationship with their customers and Jason, Jo Lennon and their colleagues demonstrate their recognition of this in abundance.

The support of my network, both close connections such as those in my three mastermind groups and also wider connections on sites such as LinkedIn, Facebook and Twitter, has also been a big help. In particular, thanks to Rob Shreeve for his invaluable advice. And to the members of The Wild Card Pack, in particular Kelly Molson, Mark Lee and Derek Bishop, for friendship, endless encouragement and for always being there.

It's usual to finish by thanking your family for their support. My family, in the form of my parents and business partners, Harvey and Claire, have actually played a more proactive role than the norm, proofing the manuscripts and offering their thoughts and feedback.

Thanks also to you for reading the book – and all of these acknowledgements!

Thank you finally to Dr Hot, for her never-ending patience and support.

Preface

They always say 'you should practise what you preach'. Who 'they' are, I'm not sure, but they certainly have a point.

I believe that referrals provide by far the most effective means of generating new business. Prospects are prequalified, they're interested in hearing from you and an element of trust is already in place. As a result, they tend to be much easier to convert than a lead generated by any other means.

I've been looking at the most effective methods for businesses to produce referrals for over a decade now. In that time I've probably made most, if not all, of the mistakes listed in this book and also followed the advice I'll now offer to you. Until recently, however, I didn't follow that advice to the letter.

Certainly I have used the techniques that I outline here. Those techniques were, after all, largely developed by analysing what I was doing naturally and what worked well. I have also enjoyed a lot of success through using those techniques. The vast majority of my business comes through recommendation or referral. I receive good quality referrals several times a week and have worked in more blue chip companies than most businesses of our size and early stage of development could reasonably expect.

The difference was that while I had been showing my clients how to develop a strong referral-generation

> referrals provide by far the most effective means of generating new business

strategy for their business, I continued to rely on my instinct alone.

The change came when I found myself under pressure from one of my fellow directors. He was responsible for generating new business and it was my job to feed him with referrals from my own networking efforts. I realised that, while we were getting a lot of referrals, many of them were for just one type of service. I wasn't strategising effectively for referrals for the business as a whole.

I decided to put my personal strategies into place and start to practise what I preached. So, I began by picking 10 people whom I felt would be comfortable referring us on a regular basis and who were well placed to do so. These people became my 'champions', the people I could confidently look to for support and referrals.

When I looked at my list it was blatantly obvious that I had been blind to what had been staring me in the face. I hadn't been asking the right people to refer us.

I ate a large slice of humble pie and continued to work through the various stages of the strategy, working out who people were connected to, what needed to happen for them to refer me and asking them for the connections. Lo and behold, the referrals I was asking for began to materialise!

most organisations can do much more to improve the flow of referrals

Irrespective of size, industry or sector, most organisations can do much more to improve the flow of referrals. Many organisations leave referrals to chance, others consider themselves to be very strong in this field.

You may feel that you already address this issue through running a 'referrals programme' or targeting social media to generate word of mouth enquiries. As I'll show in this book, these approaches often stimulate recommendation rather than referral, leaving you watching the phone and waiting for it to ring.

Businesses using standard approaches to word of mouth marketing often struggle to achieve anywhere near the level of new business that could be generated through a more focused approach.

As I will discuss, there is a huge difference between recommendations and referrals. As long as it is appropriate for you to be approaching your potential clients rather than waiting for them to come to you, you should be targeting the latter wherever possible.

It's something that people across a business can get involved in, from the CEO and their board, through sales and marketing teams, to staff who aren't even in customer-facing roles. The fact is that there are changes that all of us could make that would lead to substantial shifts in our generation of new business.

Many people feel nervous or uncomfortable about asking for referrals. There really is no need to be. If requests for referrals come about after careful consideration and planning, you know you are asking the right people for the right support and that they will be willing and able to provide it. Discomfort at present comes from either desperation or uncertainty. Both are easily overcome.

It doesn't make any difference what type of business you are in or the service you offer. Referrals are the lifeblood of businesses of all shapes and sizes. Start-ups need to bring in business quickly; multinationals need to keep ahead of their competition and bring in leads as efficiently as possible. Small business owners rely on recommendation and referral to allow them to spend more time delivering rather than recruiting; sales teams want leads that will convert more quickly, with fewer objections and prospects who will buy more.

referrals are the lifeblood of businesses of all shapes and sizes

If you sell big ticket items, the referrals to clients can bring huge rewards. If your product or service sells for a small amount, being introduced to someone who can refer people to you on a regular basis can make life much easier for your sales team.

This book is testimony to the power of referral. Many authors dream of their book being printed by a major publisher. One of FT Prentice Hall's authors, someone I know, referred me to them and had told them why they should work with me and publish this book before we had even met or they had seen a copy of the manuscript.

He connected us together and within a few days we had met and had an agreement in principle. The book still needed to be good enough, but the interest was high as a result of the quality of the introduction.

The referral to FT Prentice Hall was typical of the type of introduction on which we have built our business. Rather than send a cold proposal to a host of publishers, along with thousands of others, a warm introduction ensured interest and a meeting. From there it was so much easier to reach agreement.

There's nothing special or unusual about our company that makes us more likely to win such business. All businesses have a tremendous opportunity to grow through introductions from people who are happy to support them. Yet so few get close to what is possible because they lack a strategy that works and the discipline to keep it in place.

The aim of this book is to give you that focus and strategy.

The discipline is down to you.

Introduction

A 2010 study has shown that customers who come through referral spend more with a business, produce higher margins to that business in the early stages of their relationship, remain as customers of that business for a longer period of time and spend more with the business over time than customers who come through other routes to market.[1]

If referrals provide such powerful results, why aren't we spending more time focusing on their creation?

Culturally, we still struggle to ask people for help, yet many of us love to be asked. We'd always rather source a supplier through referral and recommendation than through cold search.

> we still struggle to ask people for help, yet many of us love to be asked

According to Grant Leboff, author of *Sticky Marketing: Why everything in marketing has changed and what to do about it*, 'In every major channel of marketing, response rates have dropped. Buying behaviour has changed from the days when consumers used to make decisions based on the adverts they saw on the television and in magazines.

'If you want to purchase a product or service today, you do one of two things – ask your network for recommendations or search online.'

---

[1] 'Referral Programs and Customer Value' by Schmitt, Skiera and Van den Bulte can be found at **http://www.atypon-link.com/AMA/doi/abs/10.1509/jmkg.75.1.46**

Proof of the rise in the power of recommendation can be seen in the popularity of websites such as TripAdvisor, where people will check to see what other people say about holiday destinations and hotels before booking. Amazon have taken this to heart, with reader reviews and ratings forming a large part of any book's success on the site and their use of what other people have viewed to guide purchasing behaviour.

word of mouth is one of the two main routes people go to

In other words, if we look at buying behaviour, word of mouth is one of the two main routes people go to. That makes it vital for sales teams to maximise their reach through referral and recommendation. A robust referrals strategy is essential to balance the lost market penetration from traditional routes.

I think that, to an extent, companies do understand this. But most of the approaches I come across are broad, generic and, to be honest, half-hearted. And word of mouth marketing still falls below more traditional routes to market in most business plans and budgets.

Large companies in particular implement 'referrals programmes' where they target their clients en masse, yet a more individual, relationship-focused approach is likely to reap much greater dividends.

Setting up an effective referrals strategy takes time and effort, but the returns should justify that investment. Much of the focused effort should come in the early stages. An established referrals strategy and culture can then lead to a regular flow of new business being generated without too much additional input.

Such a strategy is relevant whether you are a start-up business or a large multinational. The techniques in this book should be practised by managing directors as well as sales teams. Even people with no sales responsibility should be asked to participate in the referrals culture of a firm. After all, they have a network too.

Word of mouth marketing has come to the fore in the last few years, hand in hand with the boom in social media and customer review sites. A robust referrals strategy should be at the tip of any word of mouth campaign. Done properly the returns are more measurable and more powerful than any other route to market.

And yet we still don't invest the time and the resources to make it happen. You, your colleagues and your staff all have the networks available to produce the referrals your business needs.

Over these pages I will demonstrate how you can build those relationships and leverage those networks to generate the level of referrals that are within your grasp. I will show you how to develop your own Referral Book™, a system that will help you plan your referral activity and track the results.

We will look at the different stages of a referral strategy and, indeed, why you need one in the first place. After defining what I mean by 'referral', I'll challenge you to develop a clear idea of what your ideal referral is and who you most need to meet.

Any referrals strategy demands an understanding of the three core ingredients of trust, understanding and opportunity that allow people to refer you, and we'll explore each of these in turn alongside building an understanding of where those referrals might come from.

Once you know who your likely 'champions' are, both as a business and individually, it is important to focus on how you can inspire them to refer you and, once they are ready to do so, how you can make it easy for them.

Nobody can expect to receive referrals without also being willing to pass them. I'll share with you the key steps you can take to proactively refer other people in your network, something you may not feel comfortable doing at the moment.

Finally, we'll look at the tools that can help you implement a referral strategy. These include the social

a robust referrals strategy should be at the tip of any word of mouth campaign

network LinkedIn, which can be used very effectively to help you generate new introductions, and my own Referral Book, which will pull together all the threads of discussion throughout the book and help you both build and measure the success of your referral strategy.

There are a variety of exercises for you to follow throughout, to help you think about your own network and the connections you need to make.

Now is the time to invest the resource to make it happen. Set up your own Referral Book and start taking the steps to turn your contacts into champions. If you are in a larger business, ensure that everyone on your sales and marketing team understands the referrals you are looking for and how to ask for them.

track the results and make sure that successes can be replicated

Track the results and make sure that successes can be replicated, and that challenges can be overcome more smoothly a second time. Use social media, especially LinkedIn, with a clarity that ensures it delivers referrals time and time again.

The absolute key is to keep your focus. Once you understand the ideas in this book, it is fairly straightforward to build many of the actions into habit and generate some success naturally. As I discovered, however, implementing a strategy and keeping your eye focused on it elevates your referral generation to a new level.

The opportunity is there for you. The value of referrals to business has been proven time and again.

It's up to you to go out and get them.

part 1

Why you
need to get
recommended

What is a referral?

1

→ Defining a referral

→ Three steps to referral heaven

→ The numbers game – quantity or quality?

→ Tips, leads and recommendations

→ The right contacts and timing

WE PREFER TO BE REFERRED

it is well recognised that personal introduction is powerful

It is well recognised that personal introduction is powerful. I had a meeting with an individual within a very well-known trade association while writing this book. A business acquaintance of mine had sent an email introducing me to her contact, who runs development programmes on behalf of the association. The woman at the association immediately replied to both of us and invited me to get in touch.

We initially arranged to talk on the phone to see what scope there might be to work together. It turned out, however, that on the day she was free to speak on the phone, I was delivering a morning workshop at a company based across the road from her. I suggested that we meet in person after my workshop.

We therefore managed to bypass the 'prequalification' phone call and went straight into a meeting within a week of being introduced. Talking about this on the way out of a very productive meeting, she said how the credibility offered by the connection introducing me meant that she was happy to meet in person, during a busy day, without a clear idea of any agenda. She wouldn't have done so if I had contacted her cold.

You make the same decisions on the same basis almost daily. For example, how do you source your suppliers – whether suppliers for your business or those you need to help in the home? Do you pick up the local telephone directory and search the listings? Perhaps you've adapted with changing technology and now use Internet search engines or online directories?

My guess is that your preferred route is neither of the above. Most people feel much safer if they agree to spend their money with someone who has been recommended by a trusted contact. They will ask business colleagues or neighbours who they use or who they know could do the job in hand.

On New Year's Eve last year my thermostat broke down at home and I was left with no hot water. After failing to get in touch with the electrician I had used previously, I immediately contacted a friend who lives locally and asked if she knew of anyone in the area. She recommended the son-in-law of one of her friends, based on the fact that the friend is reliable and trustworthy.

It was such a tenuous link but I immediately felt much more comfortable hiring the recommended electrician than I would have done if I had picked one at random from the telephone directory. I knew that, at least, there was some comeback if things went wrong, a relationship he had that he wouldn't want to put at risk. It might not be the most rational decision I've ever made (although I must stress that I was delighted with the service I received) but it made me feel much more comfortable.

you are less likely to query price when someone has been recommended

People prefer to be referred, which is why word of mouth is the most effective route to market. You are less likely to query price when someone has been recommended, less likely to shop around the next time you have the same need and more likely to refer them on once more.

> **IN A NUTSHELL**
>
> People prefer to be referred, which is why word of mouth is the most effective route to market.

DON'T SETTLE FOR SECOND BEST

If you are serious about developing your referrals strategy, you need to be very clear about the type of information you want to receive from people. Often we are so grateful to receive support from our network that we settle for information that is much more difficult to follow up and less likely to convert into new business.

Such information does have its place and can be very useful, but in lead-generation terms it's tough to beat a good quality referral. While your champions – the people who pass referrals to you – do not make the sale, a good referral should leave you much closer to the sale than other types of business information.

One of my early frustrations when I was managing director of Business Referral Exchange (BRX), a national business network centred on the introduction of referrals, was the poor quality of much of the information passed between members. Feeling obliged to pass at least some type of 'referral', many members would pass across names and numbers of people who just might be interested in the services described, of people they had no intention of speaking to and of companies they'd had no personal dealings with. In other words, they were just *names*.

The result was that members who had received such poor quality referrals were less likely to follow up the good quality referrals they subsequently received, bringing the levels of trust in the group down.

We recognised that we needed to change this situation so we did two things. We shifted the focus in the group from the quantity of referrals passed to the quality. People were encouraged not to pass referrals unless they satisfied certain criteria and to communicate clearly exactly what type of business information they were offering.

be very clear about the type of information you want to receive from people

We looked not just at what constituted a good referral but also at other types of valid business information they could pass.

Tip

A *tip* is quite simply a piece of information, nothing more than that. No individual names or contact details are passed on; you may not even know there is a need for your services. A commercial estate agent might like to know that a company is moving; a speaker that a conference is imminent; a lawyer that a merger is being considered.

We can all be helped by knowing more information about prospective clients. With a *tip* though, we have to do all the subsequent legwork ourselves.

Lead

With a *lead* you have some more information – a name and phone number perhaps. According to Wikipedia, a lead 'represents the first stage of a sales process'. There is still a lot of work to do but you are a step further ahead.

When someone in your network gives you a name and a number and says 'you need to speak to this person', they are giving you a *lead*. If they invite you to use their name when approaching the prospect, that is simply a *warm lead*.

I once received a call from someone in my network telling me that his local Chamber of Commerce desperately needed help encouraging members to network effectively. He said that the Chamber knew this to be the case and went on to give me the contact details of the person responsible. My contact hadn't told that person in the Chamber about me, nor that I would be calling, so it was effectively a cold-call for me.

However, I could use my contact's name as a Chamber member who would like to see me work with them.

Of course, it would have been better for me if the person at the Chamber knew that I would be calling and was interested in how I could help them. But I was happy to accept the lead and follow up myself as it came from a person I didn't know well (we had met twice and he had seen me speak once), and I was grateful that he could put the information my way.

My initial call to the Chamber was not returned. When I called back the person whose details I had been given showed little interest in what I had to offer, instead trying to sell me a Chamber membership! In the end the lead proved to have little value, something that might have been different had it been taken along a step or two further.

Recommendation

Most commonly mistaken for a referral, a *recommendation* involves someone telling your prospect that they should consider using your services. Wonderful when it happens – as long as your prospect then follows through and contacts you. Until the telephone rings, recommendations hold little value, sadly.

I'm sure you've met people at networking events who like to pass out a number of their business cards to each person they meet. Maybe that's you? The idea is that you'll keep one for yourself and pass the others on.

There are two problems with this approach. One is that it relies on the other person being happy to recommend you and bring expected to carry your business cards with them wherever they go. How often have you done that?

The second problem is that if people do pass on your card to others, you won't necessarily get to hear about it, and so, if you are left in the dark, you won't be able to do anything about it either. All you can do is wait for the telephone to ring. Do you want to give up control of your lead-generation to such an extent?

THREE STEPS TO REFERRAL HEAVEN

What constitutes a good quality referral? In my opinion, there are three steps to referral heaven:

Step one – The person referring you identifies someone who has a problem you may be able to solve.

Step two – They talk to your prospect, who is interested in speaking with you.

Step three – Your prospect expects your call.

Referrals are the best form of business information you can receive. Like a *recommendation*, they are more powerful than *tips* or *leads* because your prospect knows about you in advance of your conversation. Unlike a recommendation, you are in control of the conversation; rather than waiting for the telephone to ring, your prospect is *expecting* your call.

referrals are the best form of business information you can receive

Where companies go so wrong is blindly accepting random tips, leads and recommendations when they could improve the quality of the information they receive and thus the quality of the referral. If your relationship is strong enough and someone offers you a tip, try to find out more about the potential client. If they give you a name and a number, ask if they could introduce you. Similarly, if they tell you they have recommended you, ask if you can be introduced.

IN A NUTSHELL

Where companies go so wrong is blindly accepting random tips, leads and recommendations when they could improve the quality of the information they receive and thus the quality of the referral.

After all, if someone likes and trusts you enough to share such information or recommend you, would they be willing to take the next step and make it easier for you still, with an introduction?

A very simple, but effective, way for people to introduce you is by sending an email with both parties copied in, sharing telephone numbers if appropriate. If your champion has already spoken to your prospect in advance, it should be a very simple email to write, referring to your respective conversations and making the introduction.

I'll share with you a basic email I send to people in Chapter 14.

The third step, that your prospect is expecting your call, makes such a difference. However well meaning an introduction where you can use someone's name to open the conversation, unsolicited calls are very difficult to make. When someone calls you out of the blue, how receptive are you to what they have to say?

we like to know in advance why people are calling us

Few of us can honestly admit to being completely open when that happens, particularly if we are busy when the phone rings. We like to know in advance why people are calling us and that it is in our interest to have a discussion with them. Otherwise we tend to be, by nature, defensive.

As my own experience with the trade association earlier on in this chapter demonstrates, you have a much greater chance of securing a meeting and then converting it to a sale when you have been connected through a referral. You are in control of the conversation from the beginning, have an understanding of what the issues may be and have the opportunity to do some research before calling them.

If someone is interested in my services, it is always better if I can call them when I have their information in front of me and with a clear idea of what I want to achieve from the call, rather than receiving an unexpected call from someone asking what I might be able to do for them.

I know that when I get to make that call I will come across as more professional and decisive, and can get to the crux of their issues much more quickly.

When you are given a strong referral, you should ensure that you are briefed on what they understand about how you can help them before you call, and restate the issue with them when you speak, making sure you're on the same page. If you know what their problem is and how you might be able to solve it before you make the call, you can be far better prepared to ask the right questions and suggest appropriate next steps.

GETTING TO THE RIGHT PERSON, AT THE RIGHT TIME

Fifteen years ago I used to do a lot of cold-calling. Initially in Australia in various jobs as I backpacked and then back in the UK selling advertising space for a publishing company.

One thing I quickly learnt when cold-calling was that the key aim wasn't so much about getting to the close as about opening the conversation. It was imperative that you always got through to the decision maker and didn't reveal your hand too soon to the wrong person, who would be more than happy to make a decision on their boss's behalf.

it was imperative that you always got through to the decision maker

The problem was that, particularly in larger companies, you would invariably have to get past the 'gatekeeper', in the form of the switchboard operator or the decision maker's PA.

In my various roles, many of my colleagues used to make one of two vital mistakes with these gatekeepers. Either they tried to bully their way past by insisting on speaking with the decision maker or they would make their pitch to the wrong person.

The gatekeeper's job is to screen unsolicited calls. They are not there to answer questions, so they can't help you identify whether the company has a need for your product or service. They simply want you to state your business before deciding whether or not to put you through. Most often the answer is 'no' when a call isn't expected and the anticipated outcome is a sales pitch.

Even where my calls were to the end consumer, homeowner, small business owner or decision maker, there were still strong barriers to overcome before getting my message across.

How receptive are you to unsolicited sales calls? Even though I was a cold-caller myself for many years, I still find myself giving telesales people short shrift. We tend to be suspicious of any calls from people we don't know. Many of us are time-poor, and we aren't willing to give a stranger who has called at their convenience, not necessarily ours, the sufficient opportunity to identify our needs and get us to a position where we want to focus on their message.

Now let's compare this process with being introduced by a third party. If your prospect trusts the person who introduces you, they will naturally be more likely to trust in you.

we tend to be suspicious of any calls from people we don't know

---

IN A NUTSHELL

Even if we don't initially know the purpose of the introduction or conversation, we are more likely to give our time and listen to someone if they have been introduced by a trusted colleague.

Even if we don't initially know the purpose of the introduction or conversation, we are more likely to give our time and listen to someone if they have been introduced by a trusted colleague.

There is also more chance of the timing being right, if the introduction is made when they really do have a need for your service. When you cold-call someone you have no idea whether or not they need your help at that time. It is no surprise that the return rate on cold-calls is so low.

If someone is being referred to you, the need has hopefully already been identified and you are able simply to confirm the need before focusing your conversation on the solution you provide. In addition, if the referral has been set up correctly, they are expecting your call, making it more likely that you will get past the gatekeeper.

A referred introduction also means that you are more likely to secure a meeting from your initial call, leading to the increased likelihood of converting the referral into business.

> **IN A NUTSHELL**
>
> Referrals offer us a much shorter path to market with less inbuilt resistance than other forms of marketing.

Referrals offer us a much shorter path to market with less inbuilt resistance than other forms of marketing. Despite that, I believe that most companies are still more likely to have a strategy in place for any route to market other than word of mouth. I think it's time that changed.

> **REVIEW**
>
> This chapter has covered the following:
>
> 1 Why every business needs a strong referrals strategy in place.
>
> 2 Identifying a genuine referral and being clear about what constitutes a good quality referral.
>
> 3 Making the move:
>   - looking for quality referrals
>   - the right contact
>   - the right timing.

The role
of networking

2

→ Defining the term networking and the difference between your 'network of contacts' and formal networking groups

→ The networking myth

→ The 'networking dance'

→ The core concepts of support and building relationships

'Networking' is a term that is often misinterpreted and which will come up throughout this book as it underpins any effective referrals strategy. After all, without a network, you cannot be referred.

There are two types of networking. The first type is the networking you do all the time and which underpins your referrals strategy. You have a range of contacts we'll call your 'network', made up of family, friends, business contacts, social contacts and people with whom you have a looser relationship. Without such a network, a referrals strategy cannot exist, as the people who will refer you will need to be connected to you in some way.

When most people hear the term 'networking', however, they tend automatically to think of the second type of networking – that is, the more formal opportunities offered to them by business networks, whether online or face to face. We think of strangers meeting and tentatively approaching one another, one-minute presentations or elevator pitches and the exchange of business cards.

For me, networking at its core is about the support people can offer each other, helping each of us to achieve beyond our individual potential. It's a process where we can share our experience, expertise, contacts, ideas and feedback with those who need them and where we can benefit in turn from other people's input. Networking events and sites formalise that process and create an opportunity to access such support.

> **without a network, you cannot be referred**

IN A NUTSHELL

Networking is about the support people can offer each other, helping each of us to achieve beyond our individual potential. It's a process where we can share our experience, expertise, contacts, ideas and feedback with those who need them and where we can benefit in turn from other people's input.

THE NETWORKING MYTH

It is now time to shatter a few illusions. I'm sorry, but *networking groups do not produce referrals*.

That may disappoint you if you have spent a lot of time and money joining groups in the hope of generating new business. Hours spent at breakfast meetings, lunches and chatting over canapés when you could have been watching *The Apprentice* . . . all wasted.

Before you panic and start cancelling all your memberships, bear with me. I didn't say it is all a waste of time!

The myth is that new business comes directly from networking groups. Because of that myth, it is common practice to join a group, turn up for a while and then question why you have seen no results. The fact that many miss is that networking groups are merely the starting point; most of the business done and most of the relationships built are based on the understanding developed *outside* the meetings.

networking groups are merely the starting point

This fact remains whether you are looking at an online networking group or one where the members meet face to face. In both cases you still need to develop strong relationships with fellow members and that means spending some quality time with them.

I focus a lot on the importance of the depth of relationships developed through networking. Yes, it is important to build a wide and diverse network, but the real power comes from people who know, like and trust you. That's when people will go out of their way to support you, when people will genuinely want to refer you, when people will seek out the appropriate opportunities.

Referrals and support come not from networking groups but from your network (see Figure 2.1 overleaf). As we have already established, these are two distinct entities. Your network comprises people you have

Figure 2.1   Where support really comes from

relationships with, whether they are personal contacts or people you know through business. Depending on the strength of your relationship, it is these people who want to support you the most, and networking groups are simply a way of feeding that network.

> **IN A NUTSHELL**
>
> Referrals and support come not from networking groups but from your network.

If you can focus on this, you can approach your membership of networking groups in a different way. Instead of looking for one-off 'hits' – people who you immediately see an opportunity to work with or sell to – find people who you'd like to get to know better. Spend time talking with them, meeting outside the network and developing a real friendship. Through doing so, you will soon count them as a key part of your network, rather than simply being members of the same group.

This can change your whole approach to events. Instead of scouring the room for people who might be in a related business, you can concentrate on finding 'friends'. By looking for personal connections, people you get on with, you move out of transactional mode and start, instead, to relax, maybe even to enjoy yourself. In turn, this makes you a more attractive person to other people, who are tired of being sold to, and it becomes easier to forge the relationships you are looking for.

The limitation when relying on networking groups, or online networks for that matter, is the number of people present. Unless you are in a small mastermind-style group, there is little opportunity to have in-depth conversations with fellow members and get to know them better.

This makes it very difficult to build anything other than a superficial relationship and it is unlikely that you will develop the levels of trust and understanding that enable mutual referrals and support. It is no surprise, therefore, that people who focus their networking purely within the meetings struggle to achieve the potential from their membership.

Let's take a typical referrals-focused breakfast meeting, for example. If there are 40 members present, then up to one hour of a meeting will typically be taken up with presentations. There are opportunities for brief conversations before and over breakfast. Yet there are always members who leave the meeting as soon as the formal section has finished. Typically, they then won't be seen again until the following week.

It's not much different at larger and less frequent events such as Chambers of Commerce. Many people spend time looking to meet as many new people as possible, collecting business cards. Conversations are fleeting, handshakes rushed and elevator pitches exchanged. They then move on to their next victim.

If you were looking to appoint a new solicitor, would you instruct someone just because you have met them one time at a networking group? Or would you be more likely to turn to someone you know well or who comes recommended by a trusted colleague?

> the limitation when relying on networking groups is the number of people present

'DO YOU COME HERE OFTEN?'

To move from first meeting people, through feeling comfortable giving qualified referrals and on to trusting them implicitly, you need to focus on building a relationship.

you need to focus on building a relationship

This is where many people unfortunately fall down at networking events. The first question most commonly asked when meeting people at events is, 'What do you do?' Unfortunately this is the networking equivalent of 'Do you come here often?' It's not asked sincerely, more as an icebreaker, and to be honest it's the worst time to be asked such a question – when the questioner doesn't care about your response anyway. And the reason they don't care? Because they don't know you yet – they haven't built a relationship with you.

IN A NUTSHELL

The first question most commonly asked when meeting people at events is, 'What do you do?' Unfortunately this is the networking equivalent of 'Do you come here often?'

People succumbing to the networking myth enter into a very familiar routine whenever they meet anyone new at an event. I call it the *networking dance*.

For the networking dance you first select your partner, often someone standing on their own. Approaching them you offer your hand and business card and ask them, 'What do you do?' They then respond with their carefully crafted elevator pitch.

While they are presenting their word-perfect pitch outlining everything they can do for you in a neat 60-second nugget, you study their business card intently, nod and smile politely and wait patiently for them to finish and offer you the same opportunity. Which, on most occasions, they do.

Having finished their pitch they then ask the magic, much anticipated, words, 'And, what do you do?' It's now your turn to take the lead in the dance, sharing your elevator pitch with them.

When you have both finished your pitches you shake hands, smile sweetly and promise to get in touch. Most of the time neither partner follows up, unless they are trying to sell, as no real connection has been made.

most of the time neither partner follows up

When I started networking I used to enjoy the networking dance as much as anyone. Then two things happened that opened my eyes.

The first was at an event at New Zealand House in London. I met someone there and led the dance, exchanging cards and asking what he did. He proceeded to present his elevator pitch to me and I listened politely. As he finished I waited politely for him then to ask me what I did . . . but he didn't. He simply shook my hand and walked away!

At first I felt offended, and then I was grateful. After all, he had just saved me a minute of my life that I would otherwise have wasted. He wasn't the remotest bit interested in finding out what I did, nor, to be honest, was I in him at that stage. Spending time exchanging elevator pitches with someone who wouldn't have been listening anyway would have been completely ineffective, for both of us.

A year or so later I was delivering a talk at the Scottish Exhibition Centre in Glasgow. A contact of mine from Edinburgh had come across to meet me and as we sat down for a coffee just before the talk she asked me, 'Andy, what do you *actually* do?'

I had known her through an online network for a couple of years and we had met briefly on a couple of previous occasions when she had come to London. We'd never discussed business before.

The tone of her question struck me; she really wanted to know the answer.

I'd much prefer someone ask me what I do when they are interested in the response and want to do something with it, rather than ask me as an icebreaker. Someone may ask you only once, fearing that they would look foolish if they ask you again when they really want to know.

> **IN A NUTSHELL**
>
> Launching straight into an elevator pitch is counter-productive and you are much better off building the relationship first before worrying about the details.

Networking events should be focused on identifying people with whom you have a rapport or a synergy and then establishing some common ground. Launching straight into an elevator pitch is counter-productive and you are much better off building the relationship first before worrying about the details.

I said earlier that we prefer to refer people we 'know, like and trust'. When you first meet people they aren't necessarily interested in what you do. It's more likely that they'll be focusing on what you can do for them.

If you hear advice that you should understand your USP or unique selling point before going to a networking event, don't pay too much attention. What is truly unique about you when you meet people for the very first time is your personality. Focus on building relationships first – getting people to want to know what you do because they like you. They then will naturally want to know how they can help you.

DON'T ASK

Occasionally at a networking event you may meet someone who either is an ideal client or could benefit you in other ways. The tough thing to do then is to hold back your natural instinct and pursue the *relationship* rather than the *sale*.

I'm not suggesting that you ignore very clear buying signals. One new acquaintance once said to me, 'My team needs support with their networking, we need to talk.' I would have been wrong not to respond to that.

In most circumstances though you could do more harm than good by going for the immediate return. I meet many people in professional services, such as lawyers, accountants, financial advisors and bankers, when I network. We offer a service specifically for people in those industries, so you can imagine the temptation to sell when I first meet them.

I recognise, however, that they may not be ready to buy. They don't know me or trust me at that stage and if they're at a networking event there's a pretty good chance they're not looking for new suppliers. Trying to sell as soon as I meet them would probably, in most cases, be counter-productive.

By jumping in and trying to make a sale or ask for a referral immediately, even if it's a qualified one, you run the risk of being seen as too pushy. That could set the relationship back a step before you've even got it off the ground.

Focus on winning people's trust first and ask yourself, would you prefer a qualified, loose introduction rather than full referral? Would you prefer to make one quick sale or build a long-term relationship possibly based around multiple referrals and transactions?

> you could do more harm than good by going for the immediate return

YOU WANT TO WORK WITH PEOPLE YOU LIKE

The only way those connections can work is if you develop them over time. That means taking time out of meetings to have better conversations. I often use that time initially just to get to know the others present socially. I don't walk into one-to-one meetings with an agenda unless there is a specific reason for one. I want to find out more about the other person as an individual and whether I can connect with them.

After all, you want people you like and have something in common with in your network. Over time you can then find out more about each other's business, the challenges you face and the introductions you seek.

Networking groups often impress on their members the need to have regular one-to-one meetings with each other away from their events. It's not enough just to meet once and tick that person off your list; remember that you are looking to develop a relationship and that means regular conversations and staying in touch. It doesn't have to be just two of you – you can meet in small groups socially as well.

> **IN A NUTSHELL**
>
> You will struggle to achieve anything near the potential from your networking efforts if you focus purely on the events or forums provided by the organisation.

You will struggle to achieve anything near the potential from your networking efforts if you focus purely on the events or forums provided by the organisation. Identify people who can justify a place within your network and build the relationship with them elsewhere.

NETWORKING OVERLOAD

Last year I coached seasoned networker David Baum of debt collectors Deanem Collections on his strategy. A member of several networking groups, David was attending up to five breakfast meetings a week, a couple of lunch meetings and also occasionally an evening event.

Despite this effort, he had been employing someone to make sales appointments through cold-calling and was explaining how he needed a salesperson because of the time pressures he faced.

David could point to business from his networking activity and he felt intuitively that it worked for him, but for me something was wrong. Surely someone with that amount of networking activity should not be relying on cold-calling? As we discussed in Chapter 1, he could look to cold-calling if it supplemented his other business development activity, but he was reliant on it despite a tremendous level of networking activity.

I felt that he could use his time more effectively. I suggested that on two or three mornings a week, instead of attending a networking breakfast, he should arrange to have breakfast with a key person from his network or with a small group of them.

The focus on building deeper relationships with a small group of trusted contacts should, in my opinion, bring a greater return than simply attending as many networking events as possible.

David took this advice on board and started to recognise that he wasn't valuing his time effectively. He told me a couple of months later how the new approach was already reaping dividends, with a speaking engagement alongside a Bank of England speaker and a workshop coming from more focused networking. He told me how he was now much more aware of how he spent his time and focused his activity

building deeper relationships with a small group of trusted contacts should bring a greater return

more productively, and was happy to delegate more 'cold' work to others.

it's misguided to focus on building a network before you leverage the one you already have

There comes a time in your relationship with other people when they are happy to refer you, or are ready to find out more to enable them to help you better. How many people do you know who would happily spend more time learning about your business and connecting you with people in their network, yet you've never asked?

It's misguided to focus on building a network before you leverage the one you already have. We will look later at how you can develop a clearer understanding of who you need to meet and how to recognise who you already know who is in a position to connect you.

> **REVIEW**
>
> This chapter has covered the following:
>
> 1 The difference between a 'network' and networking groups
>
> 2 The importance of having clear goals leading to focused networking activity
>
> 3 The vital importance of developing deep relationships:
>   - networking groups as a starting point
>   - one-to-one meetings
>   - avoiding networking overload.

Current approaches don't work

3

→ The difference between being 'referral-aware' and having a referrals strategy

→ The numbers game

→ Lead-generation or referral-generation?

→ Timing

→ Being proactive

In a meeting with the members of a prospective client's sales team, I was told confidently that they were 'referral-aware'. They knew the importance of referrals to their business and their sales team was constantly reminded to ask their clients for recommendations and referrals.

However, there is a difference between being 'referral-aware' and having a referrals strategy. A few careful questions later and they realised that perhaps they weren't as strong on referral-generation as they thought and a lot of potential new business remained untapped.

The truth is that even companies who understand the importance of word of mouth marketing are missing out on a substantial amount of new business. Sales are being left on the shelf simply because people aren't asking for the connections they need. Current approaches to referral-generation are old fashioned, ill-conceived and unlikely to achieve anywhere near the potential a strong referrals strategy could.

IN A NUTSHELL

There is a difference between being 'referral-aware' and having a referrals strategy.

WHO ELSE DO YOU KNOW?

Where a referrals strategy is in place, I have discovered that, more often than not, it's one that's been taught for years by sales experts. In 2008 I gave a talk to over 50 wealth managers from across Europe, the Middle East and Asia at a major investment bank. I asked the audience to put up their hands if they had a strategic approach to generating referrals. From everyone present, just one hand went up.

Before I even asked, I could guess exactly what that person's strategy would be. I knew that the wealth manager in question would be asking for referrals at the end of sales meetings. He would be asking if his prospect liked the sound of what he was offering, whether he clearly understood the benefits and who he knew who would also benefit from such a service.

I was correct. That's exactly what he was doing!

This approach to asking for referrals has been taught in sales for many years. As well as its use by sales teams, it's a core part of the approach used by many multi-level marketing (MLM) companies. The objective of any meeting is to come away with a list of prospects. This goal often seems to be considered more important than the potential client in front of the salesperson.

I met with one distributor for a MLM company who was keen to find out if he could change the company's traditional approach to 'referral'-generation. All new distributors were taught the company's system for generating referrals. Put simply, the system was a numbers game. At the end of each meeting with a prospective customer the distributor has to ask for 10 names of people who might also be interested in the opportunity. All they required were the names and telephone numbers, the distributor would do the rest.

results could be vastly improved through a more focused and cultivated referral strategy

My contact felt that it would be difficult to change the approach favoured by the company's founders. After all, it worked. If each appointment yields 10 names, of which the distributor can turn three into appointments and get 10 more names at the same time, the numbers stack up. This is *not* a referral-generation strategy. At best it's a lead-generation strategy, and in my experience they will not be particularly strong leads either.

This might be an extreme example, but I would argue that the approach detailed above is very similar to that taught in many sales courses. It produces results; if it didn't it wouldn't have lasted as long as it has. But I would argue that those results could be vastly improved with not much more effort through a more focused and cultivated referral strategy.

THE WRONG TIMING

building referral requests into the sales process is misguided

Where the existing strategy outlined above falls short is that it's far too impatient, lazy and poorly timed. Building referral requests into the sales process is misguided. At that stage of the conversation your prospect has barely built enough trust in you or understanding in your product to buy from you for the first time, let alone confidently refer you to others in their network.

Would you walk up to a stranger on the street and ask for a testimonial for your business? Then why ask prospects before they become your customers?

The 'referral-aware' prospect I mentioned at the start of this chapter felt that his organisation had a strong policy of asking all new clients for referrals. It was only after our meeting that he realised they were only asking clients for referrals once during their relationship – at the beginning, before they knew each other. Before they had established any trust.

They had no strategy in place to ask established clients for referrals – people who had much stronger levels of trust in their delivery and greater understanding of how they work. In many cases the rewards of using a product or service become more apparent over time. So why are we more likely to ask people yet to experience those rewards for referrals?

As we'll go on to explore, trust and understanding are two of the key foundations of a good referrals strategy. You need to build trust with people before asking them to refer, certainly if you want good quality introductions.

You get a different quality of referral from people who trust you. That's inherent in human nature. People are less likely to share their key contacts with you, or promote you passionately, if they haven't yet either experienced your services or learnt to trust you. At the early stages of a relationship, during the initial sales process in which so many salespeople are asking for referrals, all they have heard are promises.

Bearing this in mind, the best you can hope for from a first meeting is a name and a number. That's why I call this approach 'lead-generation', rather than referral-generation. Both are valid parts of any business development programme, but the danger of confusing the two is that your company will end up with a much less robust referrals strategy while your salespeople chase leads instead – leads that will involve more time and effort to follow up and be harder to convert.

Another reason I take issue with this popular approach to asking for referrals is that it shifts the momentum of the conversation at a key point. It's often taught that a good salesperson will make their pitch about their prospect, not about them. They will establish a need that the prospect has, explain how their offering will help solve that need and explore the benefits of such an action. That's a positive approach that leaves your potential new client with a good feeling, because the meeting has been focused on them.

With one fell swoop you can destroy that feeling and change the impression you have left by asking for referrals. Suddenly it's all about you and, coming at the end of the meeting, that's the impression that will be left. What's worse, you can lose all the goodwill you have built up, because asking for referrals at such a crucial stage in the conversation can easily be perceived by the client as though all the time it's been leading to a quid pro quo. First you try to sell them something and now you want them to do your selling for you.

you can lose all the goodwill you have built up

For the same reasons I believe that you shouldn't ask for referrals after any client meeting where the brief is to look at their issues and their business. The impact of all your support can be diminished by then asking for their help in return.

CURRENT APPROACHES DON'T WORK

There are other, better, ways of timing your requests for referrals and we will look at these in greater detail later on.

WAITING FOR THINGS TO HAPPEN

Most companies, however, do not even go to the lengths described above to ask for referrals.

Over the years I have run many seminars and training sessions on referrals strategy. I have asked many business audiences where their best and most effective new leads have come from and the vast majority will always reply 'word of mouth', 'recommendation' or 'referral'. Yet, when I ask specifically for them to describe what strategy they have in place, I am met with blank looks.

On the whole, companies believe that if they deliver good service, their customers will refer them naturally. This is a *passive* approach, and in reality quality referrals are unlikely to be forthcoming.

> **IN A NUTSHELL**
>
> On the whole, companies believe that if they deliver good service, their customers will refer them naturally. This is a *passive* approach, and in reality quality referrals are unlikely to be forthcoming.

Research conducted by Tel Aviv University in 2005[2] found that bad news travels from one person to another twice as quickly as good news. One glance at the front page of a newspaper will tell you that bad news sells. It gives us something to talk about and people do seem to revel in sharing negative stories.

[2] Tel Aviv University Survey 2005 can be found at **http://goodnewsblog. com/2005/11/28/study-people-prefer-bad-news**

This shouldn't come as a surprise to you, so why is it that business owners are prepared to sit back and expect to benefit from a flow of positive comments and referrals? There is a belief that if we do a good job then people will refer us automatically, but that simply isn't the case. When was the last time you went out for a meal, enjoyed the food and service and then told all your friends that they simply had to eat there?

The chances are that if the meal met your expectations you might have told people it was 'nice' when asked what you did last night, but most people wouldn't proactively tell as many people as possible to visit that restaurant. Yet, if you had a bad experience, you may have reacted very differently. I'll bet that then you would tell all your friends, right?

The fact is that if you want to benefit from referrals based on the quality of your service alone, you need to substantially exceed expectations and give people a story they'll be unable to resist sharing (see Figure 3.1).

give people a story they'll be unable to resist sharing

Figure 3.1   Expectations and recommendation

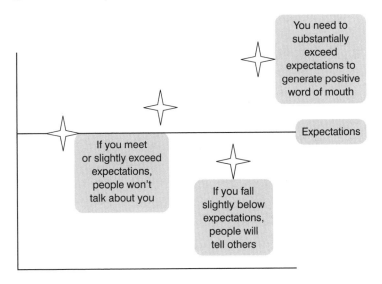

In May 2009 I spoke at a conference for the Academy for Chief Executives at Warren House in Kingston, just outside London. On the evening before the conference, Academy CEO Mike Burnage arrived with a guest. They sat in the lounge and asked the waiter for some scones. The waiter started to tell Mike that there were no scones available that day but stopped himself. 'One moment please, sir,' he said and disappeared into the kitchen. A few minutes later he came out and said, 'Chef is making some fresh scones for you now.' Twenty minutes later he re-emerged with piping hot freshly made scones.

How do I know this? Because Mike told me – he had a story where Warren House substantially exceeded his expectations. How often would you expect a hotel that has no scones to make some for you there and then?

Not only did Mike tell me, I then relayed the same story to fellow diners that night, and again I told the audience from the stage the next day.

Of course, you need to be aware of the danger that, by focusing on consistently exceeding expectations, you change the nature of what people expect to receive from you. In turn, your efforts to produce the exceptional to stimulate positive word of mouth produce tougher expectations to fulfil and a greater chance of falling below them. It's a difficult balancing act and one that you have to manage very carefully, hence the popularity and relevance of the phrase 'underpromise and overdeliver'.

A printer I spoke to about this shared his approach. 'I always strive to deliver jobs when my customer needs them, certainly never late and not before either. It may well be that they don't want me to deliver early, so my efforts to impress would be in vain,' he told me.

'However, when I know a customer needs a particular job urgently, I will pull out all of the stops to make it happen. I go the extra mile when I know it is important to my customer, not when it doesn't make a difference to them.'

WHEN DID YOU LAST ASK?

If you accept that you can't simply wait for people to refer you, you need to start thinking more proactively. When did you last ask a client to refer you?

Few people know how to ask clients for referrals and in many cases they feel embarrassed or uncomfortable about it. We worry about looking desperate, or that people will think we're struggling or that we are imposing ourselves. Yet if you've done a good job and they can see the benefit, if you've taken the time to build a strong relationship with your clients, would they really see it as an imposition?

few people know how to ask clients for referrals

The truth is, it's more comfortable to hope for a well-deserved referral than to be proactive and go out and ask for one. Sitting and waiting is not that great for your balance sheet though.

A former member of one of the networking groups I used to be involved with sold his business and went to work with an accountancy practice to help them with their marketing and business development. His first act in his new role was to write to their clients and ask a simple question, 'Would you refer us?'

Eighty per cent said 'yes', yet the amount of new business through referrals was traditionally low. This seemed odd at first, until he discovered that this was the first time the firm had ever asked their clients about referrals.

It's simply not enough to hope that people will refer you if they're happy. Unless you are extraordinarily lucky, your customers don't think that way and you have to be far more proactive if you are going to generate streams of good quality referrals.

That's where a good quality referrals strategy comes into play, and we will to look at this in more depth later in the book.

REVIEW

This chapter has covered the following:

1   Why every business needs a strong referrals strategy in place.

2   When *not* to ask:
    –   building trust and understanding
    –   being positive – focusing on your client.

3   Making the move:
    –   looking for quality referrals
    –   underpromising and overdelivering.

You can't just throw mud at a wall

→ The perils of mass marketing

→ The value of incentive schemes

→ The importance of understanding your ideal referral

→ Alternative marketing methods

THE PERILS OF MASS MARKETING

If you can't attain referrals by asking at the point of sale or waiting for happy clients to refer, what's the alternative? At the end of Chapter 3 we talked about an accountant who wrote to his clients to ask if they would be willing to refer and 80 per cent responded positively. Unfortunately, simply writing to your clients and asking is not the answer.

The accountant's letter-writing exercise simply indicated that a large proportion of the company's client base was *happy* to refer; it didn't stimulate a flow of referrals.

When businesses realise that they do need to be more active in generating positive word of mouth, they often resort to mass approaches like mailshots to existing clients, email campaigns and incentive schemes.

These rarely produce strong results. According to the Direct Mail Association's June 2010 Response Rate Trend Report,[3] response rates to various campaigns varied from 1.01 per cent to 3.42 per cent, although business-to-business campaigns fared slightly better than business-to-consumer.

To begin with, they're far too impersonal. Even with software allowing you to personalise each email or letter, people know that they are receiving a mass mailing. They are likely, therefore, to treat it with a lower priority than if you had asked them personally, or will simply file it away safe in the knowledge that you're unlikely to notice if they don't respond. After all, they're sure someone else will.

Additionally, a mailshot is a *general* request that relies upon a *specific* response. By simply sending out one mass mailing and then asking your customers to

[3] **https://imis.the-dma.org/bookstore/ProductSingle.cfm?p=0D4501 74|D1CA8598221BE6C7E964FABD9037A4EC**

talk to their contacts individually, you are asking them to do more to help your business than you are willing to do yourself.

In the case of email, there's also the risk that your messages will be caught up in spam filters before people see them, or that, looking suspiciously like a mailshot, they will be easy to spot as such and be ignored or overlooked. After all, people's flow of email traffic is frighteningly high these days and many choose to deal with important emails there and then and ignore the rest.

The other problem with general requests is that, by their very nature, they are not targeted exactly to who people know or how they can help. All they do is ask the general phrase: 'Will you refer us?'

Everyone's network varies and therefore different people will have different opportunities to refer you. For example, one of my contacts knows a lot of accountants and finds it easy to refer me to them, while another contact has a network of entrepreneurs. Rather than sharing the same request with each of them, if I ask them individually for referrals I can tailor my message to the people they know.

In most cases you'd have far more success by phoning five people with specific requests, tailored to their network, than sending out a general group email. It's easier to get buy-in and commitment from people you speak to personally and you can tailor your request to their ability to connect you, making it easier for them to follow through with their promise to help.

> a mailshot is a *general* request that relies upon a *specific* response

IN A NUTSHELL

In most cases you'd have far more success by phoning five people with specific requests, tailored to their network, than sending out a general group email.

As we'll see later, non-specific requests also have little chance of success as you are putting too much of the work and burden on the person referring you, rather than making it very easy for them to do so. They need to think about the people they know and filter their network accordingly. If you could be clearer about who you want to meet and narrow it down for your current clients, it then becomes much simpler for them to recognise one person they know and make the connection.

The only way in which I'd recommend a mass email or letter to clients asking 'Would you refer us?' would be if you then go on to use that first set of responses to identify those most likely to help you. You'd need to ask people to mark how likely they would be to refer you on a scale, and then you can focus your efforts on people who have indicated a strong willingness to refer. Now those one-to-one conversations will have real value.

INCENTIVE SCHEMES

Incentive schemes are a very popular referral-generation technique used predominantly by membership organisations such as health clubs, business associations and direct mail clubs. I personally have introduced members to the Sunday Times Wine Club because of their incentive scheme and we used to run one of our own when I was involved with a business network. In general, however, I believe that there are far better ways to engage with your potential champions than through incentive schemes.

In our networking groups we tried a number of incentive-based approaches, but the truth was our members weren't incentivised by a discount on their renewal or a cheque presented in front of their group. What really motivated them was the value a new member could add to their business, the desire to build the quality of their group. We were always more successful when we engaged with members to ascertain who they wanted in the group, allowing them to take ownership of the recruitment, rather than simply trying to reward them for referrals.

One of the dangers of incentive schemes, which we continually found out to our frustration, is that people forget they are there. Unless you offer a very powerful incentive, which is difficult if your average transaction value is low, they don't make enough of an impression on your members to stay at the front of their minds. As a result, you need to send out continual reminders about such a scheme, which can smack of desperation.

one of the dangers of incentive schemes is that people forget they are there

You also need to understand what motivates people to refer you, which means getting the basics right first.

I swim regularly at a local health club. They are constantly running different incentive schemes in an effort to encourage members to refer them. Despite this, membership is still low and they have turned to mailshots to the local neighbourhood and big discounts on membership to attract new members.

So why aren't their members referring them? After all, they ask for referrals on a regular basis and promote their incentive schemes very actively through posters around the club and through mailshots.

I believe it's because of the quality of their care, attention to detail and service levels. Rarely a week goes by without the sauna being too cold or too hot, the spa being out of order, the shower gel running out or similar oversights. For three years the clock outside the changing room showed the same time, while the one inside ran five minutes slow.

If that is the level of care they show their existing members, why would anyone want to refer someone whose opinion they respect? In the model discussed in Chapter 3, you need at least to meet people's expectations before you can ask them to refer you.

WHO IS YOUR IDEAL REFERRAL?

Earlier in this chapter, I mentioned that mass approaches are rarely effective because the requests aren't targeted. They are often too general or not tailored to who people know. One of the key lessons you should learn from this book is the importance of being very specific in your requests, and the increased likelihood of quality referrals as a result.

In order to tailor your requests, the first thing you need to do is identify who your ideal referrals are. After all, if you don't know, how can you expect other people to help you? Before you start asking your network to refer you, spend some time working out the connections you need and the requests you need to make.

> **IN A NUTSHELL**
>
> The first thing you need to do is identify who your ideal referrals are. After all, if you don't know, how can you expect other people to help you?

Before individuals work out the referrals they want to target from their champions, it is important for the company as a whole to go through the exercise of identifying their ideal referrals. Failing to look at this from an organisational level first can result in a far less effective approach from the team as a whole.

The company should not just go through the exercise but also make sure the results are clearly communicated to all staff, not just the sales team.

In my talks and workshops I often ask groups who their ideal referral is. The range of answers is interesting, but it's very apparent that few people have given the question much prior thought. It is a sad fact that most of us network to look for connections without having a clear idea of who those connections might be.

The answer is rarely as straightforward as people think either. Most businesses will offer a range of products and services, so different referrals will be appropriate for different parts of the business. Additionally, there is often a range of people you'd like to meet, and being referred to individual prospects one at a time may not be the most effective way for you to generate substantial new business.

For example, would it be more powerful for you to meet a potential introducer of a stream of clients rather than one individual prospect? What value would mentors, business advisors, sources of finance or even potential buyers of your business have as contacts? What value do suppliers have for your business? After all, there are two sides to a balance sheet.

Table 4.1 lists potential responses to the question, 'Who is your ideal referral?' Using this table, rate how important each referral would be to your business on a scale of 1 to 10.

different referrals will be appropriate for different parts of the business

Table 4.1 Potential responses to the question, 'Who is your ideal referral?'

WHO IS YOUR IDEAL REFERRAL?	SCORE (1–10)
Single low–medium transaction	
High value transaction	
Long-term client	
Introducer of new business	
Supplier	
Financier	
Mentor/business advisor	

Knowing the range of connections you need feeds your approach for referrals. Different people boast different networks and if you have a diverse network you should have the ability to connect with all the people necessary to move your business forward.

> **IN A NUTSHELL**
>
> Different people boast different networks and if you have a diverse network you should have the ability to connect with all the people necessary to move your business forward.

A mass approach to referrals doesn't tap into the diversity of the network around you. A general request can't list dozens of potential connections; you'd only be increasing the likelihood of people deleting the email or 'filing' your letter.

Instead, you need to develop a strategy that allows you to make it easy for each individual in your network to connect you to the best of their ability. Such a strategy should make it easier to focus on the real connections you need and find the quickest route to getting them.

REFERRALS ARE THE MOST EFFECTIVE ROUTE TO MARKET

Of course, referrals aren't the only route to market and I don't suggest discounting every other option and focusing purely on word of mouth. While primarily referral based, our marketing involves elements of a range of other techniques, and every business should have a healthy mix.

I would, however, argue very strongly that a well thought out and carefully implemented referrals strategy will in most cases provide the most efficient, powerful and cost-effective route to market.

Let's look at the alternatives.

COLD-CALLING

Traditionally, cold-calling is a numbers game, with a lot of time invested for possibly small returns. Much of your potential success depends on the value of business you are seeking, the conversion rates you can expect and the size of your market.

cold-calling is a numbers game, with a lot of time invested for possibly small returns

If you are selling low value items and require large numbers of sales, a mass approach, such as cold-calling, can certainly make sense, although you can still look for referrals to large distributors. Similarly, if time is a key factor and you need sales immediately, the direct approach is more effective than waiting to build the relationships that referrals rely on.

The most important factor to take into account when embarking on a telemarketing or door-knocking campaign is the cost involved. In addition to telephone costs, if appropriate, you have to consider the wages and time of the people pursuing the sales, as well as the opportunity cost of what those people, or that money, could have achieved for you otherwise. For that reason, I will always question the wisdom of allocating your best salesperson's time to cold-calling.

I recently worked with a manufacturing firm in the Midlands. The company had been losing money for the last two years, the sales team had been decimated and many of their clients had deserted them. When I was brought in they were down to three key sales staff.

One of the sales team told me that he spent one day a week cold-calling for new prospects. I asked him

YOU CAN'T JUST THROW MUD AT A WALL

how many meetings each week he won as a result of his cold-calling and he told me that a typical day's work would produce three appointments. I then asked how many of those meetings converted to sales. The return was so low he couldn't give me a figure.

I offered him an alternative that I felt would be a far more productive use of his time. I suggested that instead of spending one day a week cold-calling, he focus that time on building relationships with people he already knew who might refer him.

If he spent those hours focusing on meeting with existing clients who were happy with the service he offered, former colleagues who respected him and networking contacts in complementary industries and asked those people for referrals, how many more meetings might he set up?

In addition to generating more meetings, the proportion of those meetings that lead to a sale should increase, as should the retention of those contacts as customers. I believe that people who come to you as a result of a referral are far more likely to do business with you than those who agree to see you following a cold-call.

If the referrals are strong, your champion has identified that they have a need for what you have to offer and has given you some objective credibility before your meeting. You have to spend less time justifying your presence when you meet and can focus immediately on the prospect's needs.

Surely that person is more likely to buy than someone you have called by chance and who doesn't know anything about you, other than what you have told them.

So, in this case, one day a week spent cold-calling is far less likely to be as productive as a day spent developing a network of people who will offer referrals. This doesn't mean that you should automatically ditch

people who come to you as a result of a referral are far more likely to do business with you

cold-calling, but if it is to be used as a main lead-generation tool you should make sure that you are trained to be as effective as you possibly can be.

Andy Preston, a UK-based sales expert who teaches cold-calling techniques to teams across the world, firmly believes that cold-calling is still an essential technique.

ANDY PRESTON'S FIVE TIPS TO MAKING A BETTER COLD-CALL

'Cold-calling, like networking, is a lead-generation tool,' said Andy, 'and one that everyone should be considering as part of their business development strategy. If you're going to do it, however, you need to do it well.'

I asked Andy for his five tips for making a better cold-call.

1 **Do your homework**: Find out about your prospect by using the Internet before you call; identify areas of commonality, news or recent events you can mention, for example.

2 **Be prepared**: Get everything you need 'to hand' *before* you start – diary/calendar, list of prospects, objections you'll need to handle, call structure and so on.

3 **Don't worry about 'no'**: If your list is *very* cold, the majority of people are going to say 'no' or 'not now' to you. Remember, however, you're not ringing because you expect everyone to say 'yes', but some will so stay focused on that.

4 **Remember your outcome**: Are you trying to make an appointment? A sale? Then design your call that way to ensure you achieve your outcome.

5 **Gain commitment**: Without commitment and the person you are calling's agreement to a 'next step' your call was probably pointless. So make sure you get it!

www.andy-preston.com

YOU CAN'T JUST THROW MUD AT A WALL

What I do believe is important is to weigh up the cost of your own time and that of your leading sales team and ask yourself if there are better ways to use it. Look at the number of calls you need to make to get an appointment and how many appointments lead to a sale.

If the return on the investment in cold-calling is greater than the cost then there's no doubt that it can be a useful additional activity. You may just be better served by outsourcing it rather than letting it eat into your most valuable resources.

DIRECT RESPONSE MARKETING

Mailshots have been a staple of direct marketing for years, and over the last decade they have been joined by email marketing. The growth of email marketing, together with its lower costs, has led to a reduction in the use of physical mailshots, although some companies do still use the latter approach. In fact, as e-shots have become less effective due to high use, we may see more companies reverting to sending letters and leaflets by post.

a number of factors have diluted the effectiveness of email marketing

While they may have had a strong impact when first introduced, a number of factors have diluted the effectiveness of email marketing. Data protection laws have become stronger, making it a more expensive strategy due to the need for audited lists and the risk of heavy fines. It also means that the lists need continually updating – you can't buy a list one year and keep using it in perpetuity.

As email and its readers have become more sophisticated, so fewer e-shots are actually opened and read. Many get caught in spam filters, while others are simply deleted, opted out of or 'filed for reading later'.

Be honest, how many emails that you file for later study do you actually go back to? For many of us the growth of email traffic and the increased demands on our time mean that we are rarely willing to prioritise unsolicited mail.

If you do intend to use email marketing – and despite what I have said above, many companies do use it very successfully – it certainly pays to be creative to make an impact.

A more sophisticated approach means that email marketing has become much more time consuming and expensive to create. Strong sales 'squeeze' pages have become popular, with copy designed to take the reader on a journey that will make them want to buy. Many e-shots now make use of video technology to engage the reader. In addition, most direct mail tends to be much more effective if followed up with phone call.

You can target mailshots to certain demographics but, as with cold-calling, you need a certain amount of luck with your timing. Whereas you can be referred to people because they have a specific need for what you offer at that moment, with mailshots you rely on your message reaching your prospect when they have the need and are thinking about a solution.

When that happens it's fantastic, but the chances are there has been a lot of wastage along the way as well.

As with any form of marketing, weigh up the costs of your mailshots against the results. Marketing experts will tell you to test different approaches and find out which one has the most success. If you can find a method that brings you a profit, there's no reason not to pursue that route.

I asked Peter Thomson, one of the UK's leading strategists in business and personal growth, for his tips for any business considering using direct mail as part of their networking strategy.

YOU CAN'T JUST THROW MUD AT A WALL

PETER THOMSON'S FIVE TIPS FOR USING DIRECT MAIL

1   **Test**: Always have a 'test' in *every* direct response campaign (mail, postcards, coupons, adverts, email and so on). This can be price, bonus, time, extras, payment terms, headlines, benefits, etc. The way to test is to prepare two versions of your promotion piece (one with price A and one with price B if you're testing price) and see which pulls the higher response.

2   **Maintain accurate records**: The devil is definitely in the detail. Always measure the lifetime value of the customer/client – not just the income/profit from the first order.

3   **Follow up**: Always send a 'chase-up' email or letter to the same list of people as your original promotion (three days later) as this can often dramatically increase response.

4   **Try the 'avoid' test**: Test using 'away-motivated' headlines and subject lines (How to avoid the three mistakes …) and 'towards-motivated' headlines and subject lines (Three proven ways to …). Often away-motivated headlines create higher conversion rates.

5   **Use one-to-one language**: Always use 'one-to-one' language. Invariably people read emails/direct mail/brochures/websites and so on, when they're on their own. Avoid using 'talking to a crowd' language, such as 'some of you …' or 'we all …', and use 'you' on its own.

www.peterthomson.com

PUBLIC RELATIONS

PR has been an important strand of our business, but I feel that it works best in conjunction with other sales and marketing activity rather than independently. Strong PR complements referrals perfectly, as I have found on many occasions. Let me explain.

strong PR complements referrals perfectly

In recent years I have written for and been quoted by national newspapers in the UK a number of times. In addition, I have had articles published in a range of business publications and have a regular column in *The National Networker*, based in the US.

I can't attribute substantial direct business to these press appearances, but I know for certain that they have influenced buying decisions by prospective clients. For our business public relations has been important as a way of building my profile, positioning me as a recognised expert and boosting my credibility. When the *Sun* newspaper refers to you as 'Mr Network' and the *Financial Times* refers to you as 'one of Europe's leading business networking strategists', potential clients feel reassured.

I have noticed how many people introducing me to their contacts will refer to one or other of the quotes mentioned above. It means they feel more confident about referring me as their judgement has been reinforced by recognised sources.

Alan Stevens, director of MediaCoach.co.uk and a well-respected author and expert on how to deal with the press, suggests the following advice on making the most of your PR.

YOU CAN'T JUST THROW MUD AT A WALL

ALAN STEVENS' FIVE TIPS FOR DEALING WITH THE PRESS

1   **Be persistent**: PR is not a one-off activity. You need to raise your profile, and keep it high with a constant stream of stories, tips and information. Don't worry if some of your stories never see the light of day. Keep plugging away.

2   **Be honest**: Exaggeration and, worse, false claims will all be found out in the end. By all means use PR to promote the benefits of your products, but don't ever overclaim. You don't need to.

3   **Be interesting**: Consider the 'so what?' question. If your PR efforts don't capture your intended audience, you will be wasting your time and money. What you find fascinating may not be riveting to the people you are selling to, so ask them what they like.

4   **Be relevant**: You need to make sure that your PR message is one that is of benefit to the audience. They may be interested (see above), but in order for them to take action the message needs relevance as well.

5   **Be timely**: There's a right time and a wrong time for PR. You can 'piggyback' on another event, or you can use an anniversary. The best time to sell umbrellas is when it's raining.

www.mediacoach.co.uk

ADVERTISING

Once the undisputed king of marketing techniques, advertising has had to evolve to stay relevant to today's consumers. While broadcast media such as TV, newspapers and posters are still great places to build brands and establish product benefits, fragmentation of media channels and a greater choice of leisure activities have made it arguably harder and more costly to reach mass audiences than had previously been the case.

The flip side of the argument is that the increase in channels to advertise has made it much easier to target the ideal audience. More magazines, television channels and radio stations focused on niche audiences narrow down the demographics and drive down the costs for each, making them an advertiser's dream, as long as the numbers are high enough.

Online advertising, specifically Google AdWords and through social networks such as Facebook, has allowed businesses to target their audience even more effectively, right down to selecting the music they like, the films they watch and the books they read on an individual basis. If you're a member of Facebook, the adverts you see are there because of what you have included in your profile.

online advertising has allowed businesses to target their audience even more effectively

In an article in *The Economist* in January 2010,[4] Randall Rothenberg, the head of the Interactive Advertising Bureau, was quoted as saying, 'Facebook's audience is bigger than any TV network that has ever existed on the face of the earth.' That type of statistic underlines the scale of the change that advertisers have had to face over recent years.

Advertising online has also become more attractive since the introduction of 'pay per click'. Traditional advertising required a leap of faith, as you paid for an advert and hoped people read or watched it. Now you can advertise online and only pay if someone clicks through to your website or sales page. This does leave you open to abuse of the system by your competitors, but the positives are much more reassuring.

If you do use advertising as part of your marketing strategy, Howard Nead, business development director, PHD Worldwide, offers the following advice.

[4] 'Profiting from Friendship', *The Economist*, January 2010.

YOU CAN'T JUST THROW MUD AT A WALL

HOWARD NEAD'S FIVE TIPS FOR EFFECTIVE ADVERTISING

1   **USP**: Ensure your advertising clearly communicates that which is unique about you, your brand, your service or your product.

2   **Target audience**: Ensure you have clearly identified your target audience, both short and long term.

3   **Placement**: Ensure that your advert appears where it is relevant and meaningful to your target audience.

4   **Interactivity**: Successful advertising is highly responsive and great at starting a meaningful dialogue; ensure that it is clear to the receiver how to respond to your advert, and that you are set up to manage response and interactivity accordingly.

5   **Longevity**: Be prepared to invest in the long term. Some of your audience will want to respond immediately, others when it is relevant to them.

www.phdnetwork.com

REVIEW

This chapter has covered the following:

1   The pros and cons of mass marketing.

2   How to evaluate the effectiveness of different incentive schemes.

3   The ideal referral:
    –   understanding the importance of being specific in your requests
    –   identifying your range of connections
    –   distinguishing between an introducer and a prospect.

4   Having a healthy mix of alternative routes to market.

part 2

The foundation of the ultimate referrals strategy

The role of trust in a referrals strategy

5

→ Qualified or unqualified referrals?

→ How to establish trusted relationships

→ First impressions and your personal brand

→ Expectations, needs and promises

→ Recognising your prospective champions

In July 2009, a Nielsen Global Online Consumer Survey[5] on what influences people's buying decisions showed how trust in friends' recommendations outweighed any other influencing factor by a long way. In fact, friends' recommendations were almost three times as likely to be trusted completely as the next most influential factor. The survey found that 'peer recommendation' is trusted 'completely' or 'somewhat' by 9 out of every 10 people worldwide (see Figures 5.1 and 5.2).

Such results reinforce the importance of trust in any referrals strategy. Put simply, if you cannot establish trusted relationships with the people in your network, you will struggle to develop any strong referral streams. Although there are other factors that will motivate people to refer you, trust is by far the leading influencer.

THAT PERSONAL CONNECTION

When I started out in networking I was calling businesses to invite them to attend weekly breakfast meetings designed to generate referrals between the members. The most common objection I heard, other than the early start time of the meetings, was, 'How can I refer people I don't know?'

There's no doubt that this is a valid response. After all, as we've established, referrals are primarily based on trust between two parties – a trust that is then assumed by the third party who may be parting with their money.

[5] The Nielsen Global Online Consumer Survey on Trust, Value and Engagement in Advertising can be found at **http://blog.nielsen.com/ nielsenwire/wp-content/uploads/2009/07/trustinadvertising0709.pdf**

Figure 5.1 What influences buying decisions (a)

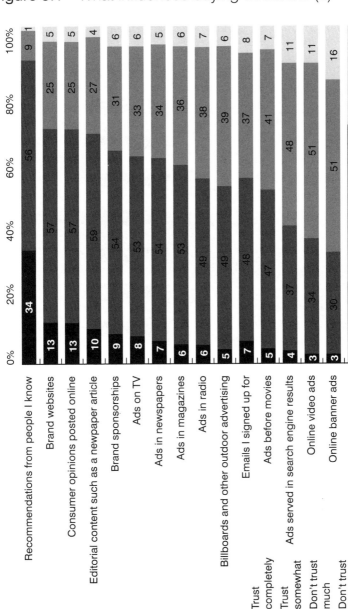

	Trust completely	Trust somewhat	Don't trust much	Don't trust at all
Recommendations from people I know	34	56	9	1
Brand websites	13	57	25	5
Consumer opinions posted online	13	57	25	5
Editorial content such as a newpaper article	10	59	27	4
Brand sponsorships	9	54	31	6
Ads on TV	8	53	33	6
Ads in newspapers	7	54	34	5
Ads in magazines	6	53	36	6
Ads in radio	6	49	38	7
Billboards and other outdoor advertising	5	49	39	6
Emails I signed up for	7	48	37	8
Ads before movies	5	47	41	7
Ads served in search engine results	4	37	48	11
Online video ads	3	34	51	11
Online banner ads	3	30	51	16
Text ads on mobile phones	2	22	47	29

SOURCE: JULY 2009 NIELSEN GLOBAL ONLINE CONSUMER SURVEY: TRUST, VALUE AND ENGAGEMENT IN ADVERTISING. REPRODUCED WITH PERMISSION OF THE NIELSON GROUP.

THE ROLE OF TRUST IN A REFERRALS STRATEGY

Figure 5.2 What influences buying decisions (b)

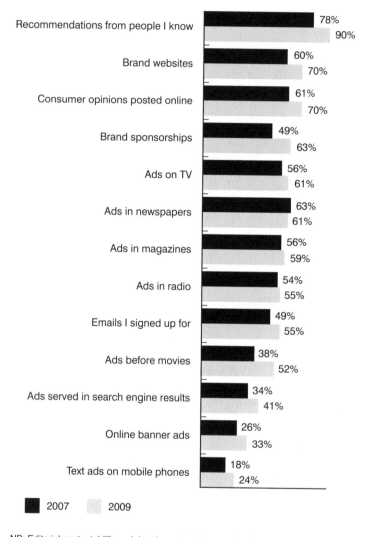

	2007	2009
Recommendations from people I know	78%	90%
Brand websites	60%	70%
Consumer opinions posted online	61%	70%
Brand sponsorships	49%	63%
Ads on TV	56%	61%
Ads in newspapers	63%	61%
Ads in magazines	56%	59%
Ads in radio	54%	55%
Emails I signed up for	49%	55%
Ads before movies	38%	52%
Ads served in search engine results	34%	41%
Online banner ads	26%	33%
Text ads on mobile phones	18%	24%

NB: Editorial content, billboards/outdoor advertising and online video ads not covered in April 2007 survey.

SOURCE: JULY 2009 NIELSEN GLOBAL ONLINE CONSUMER SURVEY: TRUST, VALUE AND ENGAGEMENT IN ADVERTISING. REPRODUCED WITH PERMISSION OF THE NIELSON GROUP.

> **IN A NUTSHELL**
>
> Referrals are primarily based on trust between two
> parties – a trust that is then assumed by the third
> party who may be parting with their money.

If you refer people you don't know, or with whom
you don't have an established relationship, there will
be natural concerns about losing trusted contacts if
something goes wrong, being made to look foolish
if the person you refer is incompetent or, worst of all,
referring someone who subsequently defrauds the
person you introduced.

If you are going to build a marketing strategy based
on referral-generation and are looking to broaden your
network to maximise the potential from that strategy,
you need to be aware of these concerns, both when
you refer others and if you expect them to refer you.

To begin with we need to be open to the concept
of meeting new people with the expectation of being
able to refer them. While a valid objection, the problem
for people who asked how they could refer people
they didn't know was that they perceived that doing so
would lead to expectations of referrals being passed as
soon as they joined a group.

Life isn't as simple as that. We can't be expected
automatically to refer people we have just met; just
as we can't operate from the basis that we can only
expect to give and receive referrals from the people
with whom we currently have trusted relationships.

After all, if there are people you refer now, then surely
there was a time when you didn't know them and a time
when you started to refer them. What happened between
those two points was that you developed a relationship
where you felt comfortable referring them. You built a
level of trust between yourself and the other party.

**be open to
the concept
of meeting
new people
with the
expectation
of being able
to refer them**

THE ROLE OF TRUST IN A REFERRALS STRATEGY

When you are building new relationships, you can still offer support and connect people while recognising that you are not yet in a place where you feel able to refer them without qualification. To do that, it is important to understand that there are different types of referral you can pass.

QUALIFIED REFERRALS

When you first meet someone, or in the early stages of a relationship, you should still be able to connect them using what I call 'qualified referrals'. By this, I mean that you are not giving your *unqualified* backing to the person you are referring, but that they still might be a useful contact.

In Chapter 1 I talked about the electrician I employed after my thermostat at home broke, leaving me with no hot water. When I asked my friend if she could recommend someone to help me, she made it clear that she hadn't met the electrician personally and that he was the son-in-law of a friend of hers.

By using language very carefully, she qualified the referral. 'I don't know him but I know his father-in-law and he's a trustworthy person,' she said. That made it clear to me that she wasn't in a position to personally vouch for the electrician, but I still felt more comfortable using him than by looking for someone in the phone book.

The key was that I understood the referral came with qualifications and took on the risk of things going awry.

You can pass qualified referrals by using language very carefully, with phrases such as:

→ 'I've just met someone who . . .'

→ 'I don't know if they can help but . . .'

→ 'I know X does this but haven't used her myself . . .'

Offer a potential solution to someone's needs while distancing yourself sufficiently from the outcome. Always be clear about your relationship with the person you are referring and the terms of referral and let the buyer take responsibility for making the decision. Always ask for feedback if business is done, though, as this will help you build the trust you need to give that person stronger referrals in the future.

> **IN A NUTSHELL**
>
> Always be clear about your relationship with the person you are referring and the terms of referral and let the buyer take responsibility for making the decision.

UNQUALIFIED REFERRALS

When you have built strong relationships with people and are comfortable that they will do a good job, you are more likely to champion their services without any qualification.

such strong advocacy requires much greater levels of trust

Such strong advocacy requires much greater levels of trust; after all, you are putting your reputation behind the referral. This doesn't happen overnight. In most cases you will progress gradually from passing or receiving qualified referrals to passing them with no qualification whatsoever.

That progression can depend on a number of factors. You may have used their services personally, know people who have and who constantly sing their praises, or have complete faith in their personality and integrity.

If you are relying on third party experience and testimonials, a lot will also depend on how well you know and trust that third party and the quality of the testimonials you hear. Stories from one or two people whose opinions you trust may be enough for you to have faith in the person you are referring, or it may be that you hear a lot of good things about them from a range of people.

When you pass such strong referrals, you would usually want to have both faith in their integrity and knowledge of their ability to deliver.

Unqualified referrals of this nature are much more likely to be acted upon by the prospect. After all, if they trust you and you speak so positively about a potential supplier, why would they want to go somewhere else? While we may be hesitant to pass strong unqualified referrals, however, they carry such weight that they play a key role in any referrals strategy.

If you'd like to be the recipient of unqualified referrals that are more likely to win you new business, you need to be prepared to offer similar recommendations to others too.

ESTABLISHING TRUST

When we first meet people we typically start from a position where we don't trust them. As soon as I say that people assume I am being negative, but I'm not.

When I say that I don't *trust* someone, it's not the same as suggesting I *distrust* them. Trust seems to be very black and white in many people's perception; you either trust someone or they are deemed not to be trustworthy, implying distrust. I would argue that reality works differently.

When you meet someone for the first time, all things being equal you will start from a position I call 'trust neutral'. Of course, the level of your trust in someone may be slightly higher or lower depending on a variety of factors such as whether they have been recommended to you, whether you have mutual acquaintances or even if you support the same sports team.

The initial level of trust or distrust can also be influenced by factors such as their industry – for example, doctors are traditionally trusted while used-car salesmen might sometimes feel they have a mountain to climb when first meeting people!

James A Ziegler, a renowned car retail expert in the US motor industry, told me: 'Traditionally people fear they will be cheated by used-car salesmen. This mythology is a deeply ingrained holdover from times gone by when these stereotypes were much more valid than today's reality.

'Although the industry has changed substantially and holds itself to much higher ethics, old prejudices sometimes remain. As soon as people see the label 'used cars' they see the old outdated stereotypes rather than the more customer-friendly safeguards and processes that exist in modern car dealerships.'

when you meet someone for the first time, you will start from a position I call 'trust neutral'

FIRST IMPRESSIONS

Your appearance and the first impression it helps you to create also has an impact on whether or not people are likely to trust you. Angela Marshall, an expert in managing your appearance and author of *Being Truly You,* believes that how you look is vital.

'Having the right image is very important as it affects how people perceive you,' she told me. 'How you present yourself, whether it is face to face with your grooming and the way you dress, to how you communicate when you speak to people either on the telephone or when you directly meet them is very influential. Looking good, being polite and courteous, having positive body language and good communication skills are key to having a positive personal image.'

It's not just your appearance that impacts on the trust that people will place in you, though. Personal branding expert Lesley Everett, author of *Walking Tall*, believes that your core values will play a vital role.

'If we build our personal brand consciously and effectively in line with our authentic core then we can more effectively be consistent with how we project it,' said Lesley. 'If we're viewed as authentic and consistent then others trust us more – it's as simple as that.

'Having a clearly defined set of values, strengths and motivators is the basis of a strong personal brand. Then you need to make sure you package yourself to project these with every communication. In other words you're consciously adding positive and reinforcing layers to your brand reputation. Others then build an expectation of you that they come to trust and rely upon.'

EXPECTATIONS, NEEDS AND PROMISES

Australian Vanessa Hall, the author of *The Truth about Trust in Business*, has developed a model to show how and why we trust and why it is so important in everyday life and in business.

Vanessa defines trust as 'our ability to rely on a person or a group of people or an organisation or on products and services to deliver a specific outcome. So there are hundreds, even thousands of points of trust in our day, every single day. And we're often unaware of those – everything from the alarm going off in the morning to wake us up, to the shower being hot enough, to the toothpaste tasting the way you want it to taste.

'We generally just trust that all those things are going to work for us and play the role and deliver the outcome we expect from them and we become aware of it when that outcome is not delivered.'

Vanessa looks at the three key attributes that make us trust.

'The first is understanding that we have *expectations*. Those expectations come from places, it comes from previous experiences, if we've had a previous experience with that person or that organisation, or that product or service; it comes from things that we read or things that we see.

'Marketing material, for example, creates expectations of what our experiences are going to be like. It comes from things that other people tell us. Referrals actually create expectations about our experience, and they come from what I call "similar experiences"; so I've had an experience with one bank, therefore I think all banks are going to be the same.

'So we all have these expectations. We often don't articulate them but we expect people to meet them and we get disappointed when our expectations are not met.

'The second thing is our *needs*. I draw on Maslow's Hierarchy of Needs to understand that from a trust point of view we buy products and services and we engage in relationships with people to meet those needs.

'What I've found is there is generally one core driving need for people, and that need drives them in all the different kinds of relationships and interactions they have. So, for example, somebody who is esteem driven will buy a car because it makes them feel good about themselves, they'll buy the clothes that they buy for the same reason. They'll engage in relationships, they'll take a job; they'll do all sorts of things that all feed that need for esteem.

'So we have expectations and needs, the *promises* are made to us by the other person, the other organisation and the other products and services, and the promises could be implicit or explicit.

'I talk about the difference between implicit and explicit promises, there's an implied promise the minute you give somebody a referral, there's a very good chance that this is going to turn into a business referral, which to me is the implied promise that can break down trust more quickly.

'there's an implied promise the minute you give somebody a referral'

'So in not being clear about that and making a statement like "this person's fantastic" or "they're a real go-getter" or "they're really friendly", you've made an implied promise and built up an expectation in that person's mind about how their interaction might play out, and if it doesn't play out exactly in the way they expect and the way they believe it was promised to them and it doesn't meet their needs then their trust in you can break down very quickly.

'Being able to trust, our decision to trust, is based on our belief that our expectations will be met or managed, our needs will be met and the promises made to us will be kept.

'So the whole purpose and the whole process of building trust is understanding the expectations and needs and being clear about those, knowing which ones are the most important to people and being very, very clear about what promises we're making and delivering on those promises.'

WHY WE TALK ABOUT THE WEATHER

I'm often asked what alternative I use to 'What do you do?' when I meet people at networking events. Only half-jokingly I tell people I say, 'Do you come here often?' I may not use those exact words, seen as a cheesy chat-up line by many, but I do ask something similar.

I might ask if they are a member of the group hosting the event, for example, or how they know the host or, if they are a first-time visitor, who invited them. Before we even start speaking I know of one thing we have in common and that is the event we are both attending, so this is a natural place to begin our conversation.

What I'm looking to do is build some initial rapport by establishing common interest. We Brits are renowned for always talking about the weather.

I believe that there are two reasons for this. First, we have a lot of it! Second, it's something we know we share. If you meet a complete stranger in the UK you can pretty much guarantee that we will have had at least one change in the weather that's atypical for the time of year, and that will give you an initial conversation point.

Opening a conversation with something that you know you have in common, such as the event, allows you to find somewhere for that conversation to develop. If, for example, you both know the same people, you may share your experiences of them. If someone is attending an event for the first time, you could ask what they are looking to achieve and find out more about their business through their subsequent responses.

build some initial rapport by establishing common interests

> **IN A NUTSHELL**
>
> Opening a conversation with something that you know you have in common, such as the event, allows you to find somewhere for that conversation to develop.

If, instead, you had simply asked 'What do you do?' and they replied 'Accountant', you'd be struggling to find the next question in the conversation unless you need an accountant, are also an accountant or are fascinated by accountancy.

In June 2009 I spoke at the launch of a new charity network alongside American comedienne and television presenter Ruby Wax. In her presentation Ruby spoke about the importance of empathy and connections in building trust with her celebrity interviewees. Where she got it right she produced a great interview, but in her earlier interviews she got a lot wrong.

Ruby explained how she failed to build any empathy with her early subjects. She was focused on getting the interview right and wanting to 'win', rather than relating to and empathising with her interviewees. 'I found myself wondering if everyone that I spoke to was nuts,' Ruby said. 'I wanted to win and wasn't interested in anything about them. It was grotesque.'

Ruby found more success when she ditched any preconceived notions about her interviewees and simply let the conversation flow.

AWAY FROM NETWORKING EVENTS

Of course, you can't build trust with people just by having the right conversation at a networking event. Trust is built over time as you get to know people personally. It's important to know each other on a much deeper level than you ever could over canapés and networking, and that's why meeting up away from events, or in the case of clients, away from negotiations and case reviews, is so important.

trust is built over time as you get to know people personally

One-to-one meetings with fellow members away from the group are essential if you want to build a robust referral network. It's only by having more in-depth conversations, both about business and about the individual, that trust can be built.

Meetings don't always have to be just between two people. I attend one monthly networking breakfast where I often set aside an hour afterwards and invite three or four fellow members to join me for a chat. I find that a group of people bouncing off each other encourages a more relaxed conversation than two people swapping extended elevator pitches.

Socialise with the people in your network as well, if appropriate. It's very easy to spot where strong bonds have been formed between people who socialise together and trust is more likely to grow from those bonds.

Warren Cass runs Business Scene, a business networking community in the UK that looks to pool various networks to make it easier for people to find the right one for them. Each year Warren organises a one-week ski trip to which he invites network leaders and well-connected people from within his own network.

One of the regular attendees is William Buist, president of *Ecademy* BlackStar, a global network based on the online platform *Ecademy*.com. After the 2010 trip William said, 'There really is a lot of value in getting a deep understanding of how others think and seeing how they look out for you when you need support. Everyone in the party of nearly 20 was either well known to each other or to someone in the group. There's a camaraderie that's second to none.

'Referrals and opportunities and ideas flowed from the general discussions, and I know that some friendships were deepened and forged which will last a long time. No Wi-Fi pretty much anywhere meant we focused on each other, and not what, and who, was elsewhere.'

You don't need to go away with everyone you meet when you network to build relationships, but powerful relationships are more likely to be forged away from networking events than at them. Attending events allows you to recognise faces. To generate referrals you need to get to know the people.

BUILDING TRUST THROUGH EXPERIENCE

While getting to know people on a personal level provides the foundation of a trusted relationship, other people's trust in you will be elevated by experience of your services and behaviour, both their own and those of others.

Testimonials play as important a role in business as they have ever done, perhaps even more so. Online networks, particularly LinkedIn, make it easy for others to leave testimonials for our services – testimonials that are easily accessed by others.

When was the last time you reviewed what other people have said about you online? Look at your profiles on social networks, on Internet review sites for your industry. Set up Google Alerts for your name and company name to ensure you know when you are being mentioned in blogs.

understand clearly what you want those testimonials to achieve

Where people have left testimonials for you, do they say the right thing? Understand clearly what you want those testimonials to achieve. If they are going to be viewed by potential clients or champions, will they take them a step closer to trusting, buying or referring you?

Last year I deleted over half the testimonials on one site because they were a distraction. However well intentioned, they came from people who didn't know me well and who simply said how nice it was to connect with me or what a helpful person I was. The ones I left talked about my skills, my expertise and what I could achieve for clients. The ones that talked about my personality came from people who knew me well and could say something substantial and relevant.

I'm very aware that my actions in deleting testimonials may sound harsh and ungrateful. I'm always grateful if someone says something nice about me. However, testimonials on social networks are part of your reputation strategy. You need to be in control of that, not other people.

LinkedIn allows you to ask for amendments to be made to testimonials before they are posted on to your profile. Don't be afraid to use that. If someone is giving you a testimonial and you know they have experienced something particularly relevant in their relationship with you that you'd like others to know about, ask them to share that.

With social networks making it so much easier to ask for and collate testimonials, make sure that they are well represented on your own website and in your corporate literature. Wherever you can, don't just share the outcome in the shape of a testimonial, tell the story. If people start to understand the journey your clients have been on as a result of working with you, their trust in you will grow a little more.

How you respond after giving or receiving referrals can also help develop trust between two parties further. In both cases you have the opportunity to build a stronger relationship, show strength in the way you lead and demonstrate absolute integrity and commitment.

IN A NUTSHELL

When you have received a referral from someone in your network, involve them and keep them informed of each step of the process.

When you have received a referral from someone in your network, involve them and keep them informed of each step of the process. Let them know when you have made contact, when you have set up a meeting and whether or not the referral has turned into business. If it doesn't work out, let them know why. If it's not the right type of referral for you, be honest. Either give them the opportunity to pass it on to someone else, or even help them by doing so yourself.

People trust you more if you involve them, if they know that you are following it up, hopefully making them look good.

Similarly, when you have passed a referral, keep in touch. Ask both parties how it went and show a strong interest on an ongoing basis.

WILLINGNESS TO REFER

It's not just about trust, though. As one of my clients said to me, your competitors may trust you but you still can't guarantee they want to refer you! When you are developing your champions, once you have worked out how well people trust you, you have to look at how willing they are to refer you.

I ask my clients to list their prospective champions and then score out of 10 the level of trust they *assume* those people have in them. We'll look at this list in more detail in Chapter 16.

One person I was coaching put my name on his list as we are members of the same network and have a very strong relationship. Alongside my name, in the trust column, he awarded me full marks.

I asked him why he had scored me so highly for trust. He seemed offended. Clearly, he assumed that I trusted him implicitly. And I do. *Personally* I think this person has as high a level of integrity as anyone I know. He always looks to contribute and help others and follows through on all his promises. Without a doubt, I would have given him full marks for *personal trust*.

However, at that time I had not experienced any of his services *professionally*. He offers a very niche service to just one type of business, and my own business is not included in that list. Without sufficient third party endorsement, which to that point I hadn't heard, I wasn't going to be in a position to trust his business to the same level.

So when you look at the people in your network and ask whether they have the right level of trust in you and would be willing to refer, be sensitive to their perception of you not just *personally*, but also *professionally*. On the flip side, if they know your business well and trust your delivery, how well do they know you personally?

Of course, this doesn't mean that I wouldn't have referred my colleague under any circumstances. I outlined earlier the difference between qualified and unqualified referrals. Referring him, I would have played up his personal qualities but qualified the referral by explaining that I didn't have personal experience of his services.

People may also be less willing to refer you if they have a personal relationship with you and don't like to mix personal and business networks. There will always be a barrier based on concerns about the implications for them if anything goes wrong. Similar issues arise when people are asked to refer to key clients or important contacts.

As well as reassuring people, you must respect their right to say 'no' if they are not comfortable referring. Also be aware of times when there may be professional regulations or other similar barriers that would prevent them referring, or that they feel may come into play.

> people may be less willing to refer you if they have a personal relationship with you

IN THEIR SHOES

If you want to know if your prospective champions will refer you, you need to get inside their heads. Picture yourself in front of them asking them if they would be happy to refer you. Imagine yourself in their shoes – how would they feel? Do you sense that they would be delighted to refer you or nervous about doing so?

One of my clients was a business consultant working with a range of large companies. When we worked together he was re-establishing his business after six months without working following an operation. He needed virtually to rebuild his business from the start.

I asked my client about the people who might refer him. We established that he had a number of high level contacts who were perfectly placed to help him, but he was very nervous about asking them for referrals.

He listed five contacts who would be potential champions for him and I asked him to place himself in their shoes and look from their perspective, thinking about how inspired they would be to refer him. I then asked him to score each of them for trust and understanding. He scored all five people we looked at high on both counts.

Feeling more confident as a result, he met with his contacts. He found it much easier to explain his situation and ask for referrals because he knew that they would be very comfortable supporting him. Just one of those meetings resulted in 10 high level referrals.

At the time of writing, a couple of projects have already come out of those meetings and one of his champions is now helping him by making introductions into Asia, opening up a new market. In addition, he has incorporated the tools and techniques we discussed into all his relationships with clients and key connections, and his business has substantially expanded since our session, almost all through referral.

HOW REFERRALS GROW WITH TRUST

Any strong referrals strategy, therefore, has to be built on a foundation of strong relationships and trust. The more people trust you, the greater the chances of them being happy to refer you, and that soon becomes a positive cycle (see Figure 5.3).

Figure 5.3   The positive referral cycle

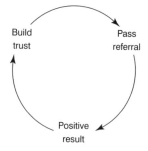

By keeping each successful referral in the loop, you will build their trust further. Make sure they enjoy a positive experience when they refer you and they will do so again. You'll see a move from qualified to unqualified referrals and to more and more business from the same source.

So many businesses I meet have people who have referred them once or twice but have failed to establish a positive referral cycle simply because they're not feeding back. They've been reacting when referrals have come in but failing to recognise the potential rewards that are available by being proactive and building deeper relationships with the sources of those referrals.

When you first meet people and the relationship starts to grow, they may choose to test you out personally or with small referrals at first. As their confidence in you grows then the quality of the referrals may get better or the flow steadier. As long as you do the right things, there will always be a stronger chance of referrals in the second year of a relationship than the first.

I talked earlier about the common question I used to hear: 'How can I refer people I don't know?' Hopefully now the answer is clear. If you want people to refer business to you, you have to get to know them first and win their trust.

by keeping each successful referral in the loop, you will build their trust further

---

REVIEW

This chapter has covered the following:

1   Making the right impression by establishing your personal brand.

2   Building strong relationships and trust by:
    – getting to know contacts – common interests
    – understanding expectations and needs
    – fulfilling promises
    – developing relationships outside the networking event.

▶

THE ROLE OF TRUST IN A REFERRALS STRATEGY

3 Knowing how to pass on a qualified referral.

4 The best use of testimonials.

5 Giving constructive feedback and keeping the person who referred you informed and involved.

Do people understand how to refer you?

→ How to respond to the question, 'How can I help you?'

→ Your ideal referral and the people and businesses who are in a position to help

→ Understanding and conveying your core message to others

→ The right level of information that will enable people to refer you

→ The concept of Problem–Solution–Benefit

Once you have established trust with the people in your network, your next goal is to help them recognise opportunities for you and have a conversation that will lead to a valuable new contact wanting to speak with you.

If you expect your champions to refer you, you need to put yourself into their shoes. A clear understanding of what they need to know in order to make the most effective connections for you will lead to a larger number of quality referrals to the right people.

> **IN A NUTSHELL**
>
> If you expect your champions to refer you, you need to put yourself into their shoes.

Ensure that they understand who you need to meet, why those people would want to talk to you and how to have a conversation about you and your services when you are absent. You need to take care not to overload your champions with too much information, or expect too much from them. The easier you make it for people to refer you, the more willing and able they will be to do so.

WHO YOU NEED TO MEET – AND WHY

A few years ago I spoke at an event, which opened with a spell of 'speed networking'. The attendees were split into two rows and they had to move along the row opposite, shake hands with each new partner and open with the question, 'How can I help you?'

Of course, having looked at length at the role trust plays in getting people to want to help, we can probably agree that the ideal time to ask 'How can I help you?' is not in the first seconds you meet someone. However, how do you answer the question 'How can I help you?' if someone you know well asks it – someone who you know trusts you and genuinely wants to help?

Surprisingly, not many people immediately come up with an answer to this question. Even fewer are able to respond with an effective answer. Most responses will be along the lines of 'anyone who needs my services' but few are more specific than that. Only a tiny minority understand how to ask for the most effective introduction for them from that person at that time.

The problem is that, although we understand our businesses and what we are trying to achieve, not all of us take the time to identify clearly who we need to meet to help us achieve those goals. Therefore, when people offer to introduce us to the people who can help, too few of us know who those people are.

not all of us take the time to identify clearly who we need to meet

If you don't know who you need to meet and the support you need to receive, how can other people be expected to do so?

When you are asked who your ideal referral is, what image springs to mind? If you are typical of many I'll guess that you're thinking of a client right now. If that's the case, let me ask you a couple of questions:

→ How many new clients do you need each year to achieve your revenue targets?

→ How many conversations with prospects do you need to have to secure a client? In other words, what is your conversion ratio?

If, for example, you need 20 new clients this year and your conversion ratio is one in four, you would need 80 'ideal referrals' in the year.

Let me ask you some additional questions:

→ Is there a quicker route to market? Are there people either in your industry or who complement your industry who talk to a number of your prospective clients and who are in a position to refer you on a regular basis?

→ If so, would they be a better ideal referral for you than an individual prospect?

These are the type of questions you need to ask yourself before being in a position to answer the question, 'How can I help you?' You also need to understand where the weaknesses are in your business that you need support with, where you can save money on suppliers and which business partners might enhance your offering.

build up a clear image of who you need to meet

Build up a clear image of who you need to meet. Be as specific as possible. What industry do they work in? Perhaps even which company? What is their job title?

If you can't refine your request to a particular company or position, you can share information about the situation they may be in. After all, people are going to need your services because of something that is going on in their business or their life. What could that be?

If people understand how to recognise those people who need your help because they are familiar with what they are going through, the problems they are facing and how you can help them resolve these issues, it becomes easier for them to make the connection.

TAILORED CONVERSATIONS

When I ask people to tell me what their ideal referral might be they always think it should be one-size-fits-all answer. But that's not the case. Should you really be asking for the same support from everyone you meet? Does everyone merit being given the same reply? Of course not – everyone is different and your conversation should be tailored accordingly.

A couple of years ago a trusted associate of mine, Chris, asked me: 'Andy, how can I help you?' I could have asked him for any number of things but I kept my response to one area.

'I'd like to increase my media coverage, Chris,' I replied. 'Are you able to help me with introductions to journalists?'

I knew Chris's background, as a former executive editor of one of the UK's best-recognised newspapers. His introduction led to a lot of press coverage, including a full page in a national paper that would have cost me tens of thousands of pounds in advertising.

Everybody brings a different network to the table with them. Having a stock response cannot account for that. You need to understand the diversity of networks around you and bring that to mind when people ask you, 'How can I help you?'

> **IN A NUTSHELL**
>
> Everybody brings a different network to the table with them. Having a stock response cannot account for that.

UNDERSTANDING YOUR CORE MESSAGE

It's often said that 'it's not what you know, it's who you know'. This only goes part of the way. When building a word of mouth marketing strategy, it's actually more important to focus on who knows you and, essentially, what they say about you.

Have you spent much time thinking about what you want people to say about you? When I ask groups this question, they almost always talk straight away about characteristics. They want people to say they are reliable, professional, efficient and other such traits.

Yet how many people decide to spend their money because they need someone who is reliable, professional or efficient? Yes, we want the people we retain to display those characteristics, but that is not *why* we are employing them in the first place.

People don't buy personality traits, they buy solutions to problems. So, if you want to generate referrals, surely you want your champions to be speaking about the problems you solve first, getting other people to recognise how your services are relevant to their needs.

spend some time getting to understand your reputation as it is now

> **IN A NUTSHELL**
>
> People don't buy personality traits, they buy solutions to problems.

Think about what people need to hear if they are going to want to talk to you with an interest in buying. What should your brand stand for if you are going to attract the right potential customers?

To begin with, I recommend that you spend some time getting to understand your reputation as it is now. Not as you hope it is but how it really is.

The personal branding expert Lesley Everett encourages her clients to contact their colleagues, clients and friends for honest feedback on how they come across. She recommends asking questions such as:

→ What kind of image do I project?

→ What impression do I make on strangers when meeting them?

→ How do my clients react towards me?

→ What recommendations do you have about my appearance to project a better image?

Such an exercise is incredibly valuable in understanding how you are perceived and whether it fits with where you want to be. From the perspective we are discussing in this chapter, I would add questions such as:

→ What do I do?

→ What problems do I solve?

→ Who are my ideal clients and why do they need me?

HOW FAMILIAR ARE PEOPLE WITH WHAT YOU DO?

The three questions I have added in the section above may seem odd for you to ask. After all, surely you should already know what you do. I'm sure you believe that those closest to you are also familiar with your business or your job. But are they?

Depending on how closely we deal with other people, their understanding of what we do may be completely divorced from the reality. If that is the case, based on the importance of understanding in generating referrals, how can we possibly rely on them to be our champions?

Very often we will simply use job titles to describe our role, or similar titles to describe our business. We then assume that others automatically know what we are talking about. It's also very easy to slip into jargon, using terms which we use every day but which don't mean much to people outside our industry or profession.

When I tell people that I am a business networking strategist I probably leave them looking blank!

people will simply switch off if they don't understand what we mean

The danger is that people will simply switch off if they don't understand what we mean. Many people will be too embarrassed to ask for clarity, particularly more than once. They are more worried about looking foolish. Instead, they will change the subject and lose interest.

Bearing this in mind, if someone does show enough interest to quiz you on what you do, or what you mean, be gracious and patient in response. Such patience may pay off.

A couple of years ago I was approached by one of my connections on *LinkedIn*, who asked me to introduce him to someone in my network. Both parties were involved in finance, but I didn't understand his jargon-filled explanation of why he wanted to be introduced, so I didn't feel comfortable making the connection.

I went back to him and explained my problem. I asked him if he could repeat the request in a format that I could understand. His response was somewhat curt and unhelpful, suggesting that his explanation was straightforward enough. Suffice to say, he didn't get the introduction.

If people want to understand what you do in order to help you more effectively, make it easy for them to do so rather than antagonise them. After all, you are the one who stands to benefit.

WHO DO YOU WANT THEM TO SAY IT TO?

Once your network understands what you want them to say about you, you then need to focus on who you want them to share your message with. If, for example, you are looking for contacts in the public sector, there is little advantage to be gained if your message is being shared with small start-up companies.

Table 6.1   Who influences your prospects?

WHO DO YOU WANT TO MEET?	WHO ARE THE KEY INFLUENCERS IN THEIR INDUSTRY?	WHO DO YOU KNOW WHO CAN INTRODUCE YOU TO AN INFLUENCER?

Think of your ideal referral and write down a list of people or companies you would love to meet (see Table 6.1). You should have a clear idea of the groups of people and businesses you want to reach and who they might be listening to.

focus your networking on building influential connections

The people they are listening to may be the key for you. Rather than targeting individual sales direct, focus your networking on building influential connections. Who are the key influencers in your arena and how can you get in front of them?

Start by considering your existing network. Who is talking to the people you most want to meet? They are the people you need to be spreading your message.

Before you do this, ask yourself why they would want to build a relationship with you. If they are the most influential people in their field, many people will be looking to meet and influence them. Why should you stand out from the crowd? Why would they want to associate with you?

Once you have made the connection, supporting them in what they are trying to achieve will help. Find out their key goals and provide good and appropriate connections, timing them for the best impact.

But you need to be known by them first to do that. Being seen as an influencer and expert in your own right certainly helps. Using social media to raise your profile and establish your credibility and expertise may bring you on to their radar.

HOW YOUR CHAMPIONS RECOGNISE THE OPPORTUNITY TO REFER YOU

Before asking someone to make introductions on your behalf, ask yourself two things:

→ Who do they know?

→ How do they know them?

Don't waste the opportunity for someone to refer you by asking for introductions to people they are unlikely to know or to meet. Instead, think about the people they deal with day to day, either as clients or suppliers, or other people they come across.

If you know a person well, you may know more about what their spouse does, about their neighbours, friends and family. I'm not suggesting you either stalk or interrogate them (and I certainly hope you wouldn't!) but, as we have already seen, opportunities can arise through a range of different relationships.

Think of five people from across your network – clients, suppliers, friends or family. Who would they naturally talk to as part of their professional life? Do you know what their family or friends do? I'll tell you later in the book about a bank manager who introduced me to the sales director of a major airline because he coached the sales director's son in a children's football team. What similar 'hidden' connections do the people in your network have?

Using Table 6.2, make a list of the connections in your network and start to picture who is in their network.

Table 6.2 Who does your network know?

NAME OF CONTACT	YOUR RELATIONSHIP	WHAT DO THEY DO?	WHO DO THEY DEAL WITH IN THEIR JOB?	WHO IS IN THEIR PERSONAL NETWORK?

The key reason I raise this is to encourage you to think about the conversations your contacts have with your prospects and how likely they are to recognise an opportunity for you. It can be very tempting only to consider someone's professional experience and contacts when asking for a referral from them and to couch our request in professional terms.

Yet, if you are explaining your ideal prospects' needs in purely business terms, someone who is a family member or friend may not be having a sufficiently in-depth conversation with them to allow them to recognise the opportunity for you. In fact, because you are focusing on their business relationships, they may not even realise they have the ideal person to introduce you to in their cousin, golf buddy or next door neighbour!

In a recent conversation one of my potential champions mentioned, in passing, what her husband does for a living. She only mentioned it because where he works is close to where I live, yet he is potentially an excellent connection for me, possibly the perfect

think about the conversations your contacts have with your prospects

client. It hadn't occurred to her before because the conversations we have had have been focused around a different marketplace, one where she personally has years of professional experience.

WHY DO PEOPLE NEED YOUR SERVICES?

Focus on a few of your current customers, those who you'd like to replicate by meeting people or companies with similar needs.

IN A NUTSHELL

Look back at your past successes and work out what led that client to hire you. Translate that into a compelling message for your contacts to communicate when they meet a prospect for you.

Look back at your past successes and work out what led that client to hire you. Translate that into a compelling message for your contacts to communicate when they meet a prospect for you.

For example, if you are an IT consultant, while friends and family of your prospect may not know that they are looking for more advanced technology solutions, they may know when that person is looking to move their business from a home office into commercial premises and employ more staff. The chances are that, at that stage, they will need some more advanced technology such as an exchange server and networked computers.

Put simply, make it as easy as possible for the potential champions in your network to refer you by painting pictures of the people you help in undemanding terms that everyone can understand,

and by using their behaviour and activity to outline reasons why they are likely to need your help.

Using Table 6.3, think about the reasons why people buy from you. This will make it easier for you to communicate this information to your potential champions.

Table 6.3   Why do people buy from you?

NAME OF CLIENT	WHAT SERVICES HAVE YOU PROVIDED FOR THEM?	WHY DID THEY NEED YOUR SERVICES?	HOW WOULD THEIR NETWORK HAVE RECOGNISED THE NEED?

ASKING THE RIGHT QUESTIONS

To help you open up people's minds to their full network, you have to ask the right questions. The format used across networking groups for years has been the ideal phrase: 'Who do you know who …?'

It is powerful because it's an 'open' rather than 'closed' question. It doesn't allow for a 'yes' or 'no' response, which 'Do you know anyone who …?' does. Instead it assumes a positive response and forces people to think before answering. Compare this to the oft-used 'If you know anyone who …', which doesn't even require a response at all!

If you're assuming a positive response, my advice would be to create the circumstances where there's a

target your request where you know there will be a positive answer

strong chance you'll receive one. Target your request where you know there will be a positive answer. That comes from understanding the network of the person you're asking.

Who will your contacts know, and will they understand your prospect's business or situation well enough to recognise the problem they are experiencing and how you can help solve it?

Don't make your request too broad or your champions will need to wrack their brains trying to remember which of your services or products would be perfect for the prospect. If doing this is too much of an effort, your champions will not be prepared to do so and will probably choose not to bother.

When I ran networking groups we used to have a lot of members from various companies who provided low-cost telephone calls and general utilities such as gas and electricity. More than once I witnessed someone representing such a company stand up in front of a networking group and ask for 'anyone who has a telephone'. Needless to say, each time I saw that happen the person making the request went home empty handed and downhearted.

The reason was simple. The request was too broad. How many people do you know who own a telephone? I think it's fair to suggest that the answer is a lot, too many in fact for you to come to a specific response.

If that is the case, how would you respond to such a request? Would you be willing to introduce that person to everyone you know who has a phone? It's unlikely as this would be a huge task that would take you too much time.

In which case, how do you decide who to introduce them to? You have to think about a very large network and pick individuals from it, yet you have no real criteria to help you make the selection. Again, this is a huge task, which you're unlikely to approach with much enthusiasm.

What could the utilities person have done instead? The answer is to have been more specific in their request – for example, asking instead for connections to retired people on a tight budget and with relatives living far away, and so needing to save money on their phone bills.

Do the filtering for your champions. Be specific about the referrals you want and make their job so easy to do that it becomes automatic.

IN A NUTSHELL

Do the filtering for your champions. Be specific about the referrals you want and make their job so easy to do that it becomes automatic.

The moment that I ask you whether you know anyone with an elderly parent living alone and not in care, your subconscious would leap into action and, if you know someone who fits the bill, pull up a picture of them in your mind.

If I ask you who you know who has either just gone to university or has children who are on their way to university, if you know someone you'll think about them now. I'm doing the filtering for you.

If I ask you who you know who's just had a baby, if you know someone they will jump into the forefront of your mind. Again, I'm doing the filtering for you.

The beauty of this approach is that I can decide what to ask you for based on my knowledge of your age, background and the circles you mix in. I might ask an 18-year-old who they know who has gone to university, a 30-year-old who they know who's had a baby and someone in late middle age who they know who has an elderly parent. Through such steps I increase my chances of a positive response.

PAINTING PICTURES

As we have seen, the flow and the quality of referrals that you receive depends a lot upon the quality of the message you communicate to your network and, in particular, their ability to spot ideal opportunities to introduce you. Having recognised the opportunity, your champions then need to be able to raise the prospect of a conversation with you and get the other party interested in taking your call.

Many people will find it easier to refer you if you can help them to visualise the person you want to meet in their mind. Paint pictures for people by being very specific in your descriptions of who you are looking to meet.

the narrower the request you make, the clearer the picture you will paint

The narrower the request you make, the clearer the picture you will paint, as long as your champions know them, which, if you've done your homework properly and tailored your request appropriately, they should do.

Breaking the message into bite-sized chunks and giving it a clear structure gives you more impact. For referrals the simplest model to use is *Problem–Solution–Benefit*.

→ What is your prospect's *problem*?

→ How will you *solve* it?

→ How will they *benefit* as a result?

If you can get those points across clearly, people should find it very straightforward to make connections for you.

Don't underestimate the power of telling stories to get your message across. In over a decade of networking I have seen the impact time and again of people getting their point across by describing how they helped a particular customer and the

THE FOUNDATION OF THE ULTIMATE REFERRALS STRATEGY

outcome. People respond to stories that make them laugh, stories that frighten them, stories that have a particularly happy outcome.

What have you done for a client that has had a huge impact on their business? What would have happened if you hadn't been involved? Is there a story to be told? You don't have to breach a confidence, just share the key points.

I've also seen a lot of people fail to get their message across and make minimal impact because they've focused too much on the theory of what they do and have overloaded people with jargon, rather than illustrating it with practical examples.

At one workshop, my clients showed me the results of their board's marketing brainstorm the evening before. They had decided to work on a single statement about what they do, their elevator pitch. After much discussion they came up with the following:

What do we do?

Full stack systems integration for the UK mid-market delivering rapid business change using advanced technology.

What does this mean to you? If you're not in the same industry, or a related business, the chances are that it will mean very little. Interestingly, this only represents one part of their business, yet they came up with this summary of their activity as a whole. It is overloaded with jargon, with their own perspective and assumes a high level of understanding.

I have a problem with terms like 'mid-market', 'business-change' and even with 'networking'. They all assume a certain level of understanding. Yet if people aren't involved in your business they may have a different perspective on, or understanding of, those

explain your business in simple language

terms. It's so important to explain your business in simple language, so that a child can understand it, if you want others outside your business or your industry to help you.

The first time I worked with this client I found myself travelling to their offices realising that, despite several meetings and conversations, I still didn't understand what they did. When I got to their offices I started to read some case studies of work they had done for their clients.

Reading these stories, which outlined the problems their clients had faced, the solution provided and the benefits enjoyed as a result, suddenly made everything clear.

IN A NUTSHELL

Ask yourself whether your message is sticky, memorable and transferable.

Ask yourself whether your message is sticky, memorable and transferable. Does it stick in people's mind to the extent that they recall it when they need to? Will they be able to remember the key points you need them to get across? Can they explain it to your prospect in a way that is both understandable and promotes action?

Chip and Dan Heath, in their excellent book *Made to Stick*, explain what is important about a story that sticks: 'We understand it; we remember it and we can retell it later.'[6]

Ultimately your aim is for your champion to be able to recognise the person who needs your help, understand their problem, feel confident about raising the subject and make the introduction.

[6] Chip and Dan Heath (2008), *Made to Stick*. Arrow Books.

ELICITING A RESPONSE FROM THE PROSPECT

The Problem–Solution–Benefit model is the key to help your champion prepare for such conversations. It's easy to remember and easy to repeat to others. If you've done your preparation well, it should also lead to your prospect recognising that it is in their interests to speak with you and to become interested in the referral.

To help illustrate this, I spoke with Mikael Arndt, CEO of Arndts, a sales training company in Stockholm. I asked Mikael to outline a key potential client and then went through the Problem–Solution–Benefit model with him for that prospect.

Mikael is keen to meet sales directors who manage a team of at least five sales representatives.

> **Problem** – The sales directors may be complaining that their salespeople do not get enough out of customer meetings, aren't assertive enough or that they don't spend enough time meeting with their customers.
>
> **Solution** – Most salespeople know what to do but they don't do it because they are not as goal oriented as they should be. Mikael's training involves recording the sales team in actual client calls and then analysing the calls together with them.
>
> **Benefit** – When the salespeople hear themselves in their calls, they realise how they have been underperforming and Mikael helps them work through the key steps they can take to raise their game.

I also talked earlier about how case studies help to put theory into context and make your message so much more memorable and transferable. Once you've helped your champion understand how to recognise the right people for you to meet and how you can help them, share a story where possible of a similar situation in the past. Talk about what your client's problem was, how you solved it and the end result for your client. It's Problem–Solution–Benefit wrapped into one tidy package.

In Mikael's case, he told me how he had recently worked with a company who were complaining that their sales team were not making enough calls and weren't looking to improve themselves either. They didn't seem to care as they were earning a sufficient salary without doing much.

Mikael started by showing the sales team how a call should be made, and each phase therein. Everyone thought that they were already doing everything he talked about. However, when they listened to the live calls Mikael had asked them to tape, they could recognise that they weren't performing to the level they had thought.

As a result of recognising these shortfalls, the sales team became more receptive to Mikael's training and other self-development, as well as applying the lessons learnt. The company concerned tripled their sales over the next four weeks.

Using a story such as Mikael's incorporates all three elements of Problem–Solution–Benefit but in a way that brings the theory to life. People who hear Mikael's story are more likely to feel comfortable referring his company, and recognise the opportunities to do so, than if he just said he wanted to talk to anyone who needed sales training.

The key is that they would find it easy to recall his story and the key elements and repeat it well enough to generate the prospect's interest in a further conversation.

ASK YOUR NETWORK

Of course, you could simply ask your champions what they'd need to know to refer you! I wouldn't launch into this as your first question. By this stage you should be aware of the importance of building relationships first, but when trust is at the right levels and you know people are comfortable referring you, why wouldn't you?

When you respond, bear in mind the advice above and keep it simple, painting pictures for them. But if they guide you with the information they feel they need to know, people will feel more confident about passing you referrals.

REVIEW

This chapter has covered the following:

1 Ensuring your message is simple and focused.

2 Making sure your message is tailored so that it is relevant to your potential referrer and their contacts.

3 Ensuring your champions are able to recognise referral opportunities for you.

Who has
the best
opportunity
to refer you?

→ How to recognise potential introducers

→ Standing out from the crowd

→ Establishing your niche market

→ Making competition and synergy groups work
  for you

As previously indicated, identifying those people who are well placed to refer you, either because of their understanding of your marketplace or owing to their exposure to your prospective clients, will help you develop strong sources of new opportunities.

People who understand your marketplace are able to speak the same language and recognise opportunities for you with ease. As hard as you may work to make your wider network aware of who you help and how, those with experience of what you do will always have a greater depth of understanding.

> **IN A NUTSHELL**
>
> People who understand your marketplace are able to speak the same language and recognise opportunities for you with ease.

A graphic designer, for example, may find it much easier to generate referrals from printers and website developers than from someone not involved in a related industry.

I'm not suggesting that you simply write off people who want to refer you, understand how to but who might not be speaking with the right people. However, once you have confirmed that they really don't have the opportunities to refer you, it may be better to focus your attention elsewhere.

At the beginning of a referral strategy coaching programme I asked one of my clients to identify five people who he felt would be good champions for him. By the third session it became clear that one of the five was simply not in a position to refer regularly. He had spent a lot of time with her, succeeded in building her trust, but she was not having the conversations that would lead to referral opportunities frequently enough.

He quickly came to the decision to keep in touch with her but to focus his referral strategy activity elsewhere. It would be very difficult commercially to justify the time invested in building the relationship with her in terms of the referrals she would be in a position to provide.

STANDING OUT FROM THE CROWD

Think about former colleagues or competitors who have moved on to other roles, suppliers who specialise in your market or complementary businesses sharing the same customer base, for example.

If you want to get the edge on your competitors, you need to be creative about this. There will be obvious introducers in your industry that everyone approaches. For example, within professional services there exists what I call 'the Holy Quadruplicate' of solicitors, accountants, financial advisors and banks.

Depending upon their area of expertise (for example, property lawyers may look more to architects and surveyors for introductions), when asked who is most likely to refer them, each of the four professions above will typically mention the other three. After all, they tend to be talking to similar clients with similar issues but have different expertise. They are also all in positions where they are trusted by their clients. That means that each of the four is continually being approached by the others with a view to establishing a referral relationship.

You can still stand out from the crowd when looking for referrals from obvious sources. As we have discussed, few of your competitors will have a referrals strategy, and if they do, depending on the industry, they are unlikely to be focused on building deep relationships. While your competitors may approach introducers occasionally, you can be speaking to them

if you want to get the edge on your competitors, you need to be creative about this

WHO HAS THE BEST OPPORTUNITY TO REFER YOU?

continually, getting well known within their companies and winning their loyalty.

If you can think differently from your competitors, however, you can identify potential sources of referrals who they will never think of. There are a couple of approaches that will help you identify less obvious introducers.

THE PROCESS AND THE PEOPLE

Why do people buy your products or services? What has driven that need?

Depending on the nature of your business, the chances are that you are part of a bigger process driven by a change in their business or their life. Needs arise often out of change and those changes can drive more than one need.

IN A NUTSHELL

Needs arise often out of change and those changes can drive more than one need.

Imagine, for example, that you install telecom systems for a living. You may have customers who need your services because they are moving offices. The process they are involved in, moving offices, demands more services than just a new phone system.

Those customers may also require the services of commercial estate agents, property lawyers, surveyors, architects, office furniture providers, an office stationery company, printers, sign writers, IT network engineers, contract cleaners and more.

All these businesses are talking to potential customers of yours at a time when they are most likely to need your help. Therefore, all those businesses are potential champions for your business. They have the opportunity to refer you and are in a position to do so, just as the need arises.

Some businesses will be better placed than others to refer you, others will be more trusted. In the example above, the IT network engineer or the architect are probably best placed to refer the telecoms company owing to their relevant and trusted expertise or the appropriate timing of their work.

Run through this exercise as you consider your own business. Above is just one example of why someone might call in a telecom systems provider. List every reason why someone uses your products or services and why that reason may have come about. Then try to identify as many companies as possible who also service that need.

Once you have done that you will start to identify the types of company that come up time and again. Those will be the people you most want to speak to and try to come to a referral relationship with.

An additional benefit of this exercise is that it will help you to recognise areas of industry or the types of client in whom you specialise. Once you are aware of your niche markets, it becomes an effortless step to identify other suppliers to those markets with whom you can develop a cross-referral relationship. As your reputation in that market grows, so other suppliers will want to work more closely with you.

Another approach is to think of the people you deal with within your client companies and identify who else deals with people in that position. If, for example, you tend to deal directly with the finance director of an organisation then, if you can identify who else deals with finance directors, you know that they are in a position to refer you. As with the example above, look for those who are most trusted and whose advice is most relevant to what you do.

some businesses will be better placed than others to refer you

WHO HAS THE BEST OPPORTUNITY TO REFER YOU?

COMPETITIVE ADVANTAGE

Your competitors are another group of people with the ideal opportunity to refer you – a group that is often automatically overlooked. After all, why would your rivals refer you?

there are many examples of competitors working together and feeding each other's businesses

However, there are many examples of competitors working together and feeding each other's businesses. Many believe that having strong competitors boosts their own business by raising both the profile of and standards in their industry.

Cavett Robert founded the National Speakers' Association in the US in 1972. At the time only a small proportion of organisations in the US used outside speakers. Robert wanted to change that, both by raising the quality within the speaking profession and by raising awareness of speaking as a profession itself.

He had a vision of an organisation where speakers could improve their performance and their business through shared knowledge, encouragement and experiences. His motto was 'don't worry about how we divide up the pie, there is enough for everybody. Let's just build a bigger pie!'

Additionally, there are a number of reasons why you might want to refer competitors, and why they might be willing to refer you. You may not be best positioned to look after a client's needs because of location or the expertise required, for example. In such cases it is arguably better to refer them to a competitor and retain their goodwill for the future than either to provide a poor service or to apologise and leave them to source their own solution.

Establishing a referral relationship with your competitors can also offer you economies of scale. Many business consultants and trainers will create a system of associates to help them take on contracts that may otherwise be too large, or develop regionally or internationally when they are unable to travel. Outside of that associate relationship they may still compete with the people with whom they work closely at other times.

If you understand who deals with your market and how they fit with your own offering, you can set up a series of collaborations and joint ventures that will see businesses that otherwise compete with you bring customers to your door.

SETTING UP SYNERGY GROUPS AND NETWORKS

It's not enough to recognise the people to whom you can potentially turn for referrals. Later in this book we will look more closely at how you turn those contacts into champions.

Unfortunately I have come across many cases where companies manage to work out who could refer them but then sit back and wait for things to happen. Unsurprisingly, nothing does. If you want a successful referrals strategy it's vitally important that you are *proactive* rather than *reactive*.

> it's vitally important that you are *proactive* rather than *reactive*

While there are many examples of joint-venture exercises and complementary business co-promotions designed to increase the quantity of referrals between businesses, even these often tend to be forgotten once established.

If the directors of two firms meet at networking groups regularly and agree to cross-refer, how often does that relationship extend to other staff at both companies? If you have a successful meeting and set up an agreement with another firm to cross-refer, what are the chances of success if you don't keep on meeting regularly?

For a successful referral partnership between two firms to really take hold, it needs to have sticking power and to become part of the culture of both firms.

> **IN A NUTSHELL**
>
> For a successful referral partnership between two firms to really take hold, it needs to have sticking power and to become part of the culture of both firms.

We have been running a programme over the last year for professional services firms precisely to teach how to build long-lasting relationships between people from different firms. In the programme we bring together five people from each of three firms, usually a law firm, accountancy practice and one other complementary business, such as insurance brokers, financial advisors or banks.

The groups meet regularly over the course of a year and build their referral strategies together, working in groups of three, one from each firm. Through this they all get to know each other better, understand what the other firms are looking for in terms of referrals and start to recognise opportunities for each other. What's more, as relationships build they find that they want to help each other and start looking proactively for introductions.

Taking this to another level, I have seen a number of new ventures and strategic alliances arise from referral relationships between firms. Clearly there need to be strong synergies between the partner businesses for this to be a success.

One such venture is Q&A People Matter, a collaboration between two London-based firms – financial management consultancy Ablestoke

Consulting and HR and employee benefit consultants Quin~essence.

Having initially met at a networking event at Ablestoke's offices, the mutual rapport was such that a follow-up lunch meeting was quickly arranged and the principals of the two firms immediately started exchanging introductions and looking for opportunities for each other.

The two companies soon recognised that they shared a commonality of purpose and that there was a gap in the marketplace they were well placed to fill. Following advice from a third party they set up a joint marketing brand in 2010.

Neil Mutton, the managing director of Ablestoke, shared the reasons for this success with me. 'Beyond the "mutual likeability", which is always the first positive signal when networking, there is a real honesty and similarity of personal styles of the management of both companies,' he explained.

'It transpires that the businesses are culturally aligned, management are driven to achieve the same goals, have complete trust in the other and that, in addition, we both operate and "share" in a very honest and transparent manner.

'Of course it's a major benefit if there is a business synergy beyond the odd referral, which in this case there is: the "joined up" offering works to the mutual and equal benefit of both companies. In fact both companies feel they are getting the better deal – so a perfect match.'

The alliance has had a positive impact on the ability of the staff across both firms to recognise opportunities for each other.

'Staff of both companies now have a much wider range of services to offer, so networking becomes more confident and much easier,' Neil continued.

'The first new client of Q&A PM came from an international HR "need" that the client had identified. There is no way that this conversation would have happened had it not been for the collaboration Ablestoke had with Quin~essence and the additional range of services offered across the companies.'

Traditionally many people prefer to keep their competitors at a distance and instead seek new business opportunities from networking events. If you can open your mind to the benefits that collaboration can bring, you create a sea of opportunities that may not have been there before. Sometimes being referred to a potential competitor could be the best opportunity to open up your business.

REVIEW

This chapter has covered the following:

1   Where your key connections are and how to develop those relationships.

2   Guidelines on how to optimise your network's contacts.

3   Techniques to generate more business by cross-referral.

part 3

How your network can help you generate referrals

The six degrees of separation and how they influence your referrals strategy

→ The six degrees of separation

→ A manageable network

→ Building a diverse network with strong relationships, deep enough to make a difference

→ Growing your network

THE SIX DEGREES OF SEPARATION

As you develop your referrals strategy, your focus has to shift from the standard view of selling to the people in your network and on to understanding how to sell through them. To be able to recognise the potential this approach offers, there are few better places to begin than with the theory of six degrees of separation.

The theory was initially popularised in a 1929 short story called 'Láncszemek' or 'Chains' by the Hungarian writer Frigyes Karinthy. One of the characters in Karinthy's story bet a group around him that they could name 'any person among earth's one and a half billion inhabitants and through at most *five* acquaintances, one of which he knew personally, he could link to the chosen one.'

Taking up the challenge, the character immediately finds a path from himself to a Nobel Prize winner. He demonstrates that he knows a tennis champion who plays tennis with the Swedish King Gustav, who presents the Nobel Prize and who must, therefore, know the Nobel Prize winner.

Finding connecting celebrities to be trouble-free, the character then takes on a more difficult challenge – finding a path through to a worker in the Ford factory:

> *The worker knows the manager in the shop, who knows Ford; Ford is on friendly terms with the general director of Hearst Publications, who last year became good friends with Árpád Pásztor, someone I not only know, but is to the best of my knowledge a good friend of mine – so I could easily ask him to send a telegram via the general director telling Ford that he should talk to the manager and have the worker in the shop quickly hammer together a car for me, as I happen to need one.*[7]

[7] Frigyes Karinthy (1929) 'Chain-Links'. In Mark Newman, Albert Lasio-Barabasi and Duncan J. Watts (eds) (2006) *The Structure and Dynamics of Networks*, 21–6. Princeton University Press.

Unaware of this story until recently, whenever I have talked about six degrees of separation in the past, I have credited Professor Stanley Milgram with its discovery. This is despite the fact that Milgram himself never used the term.

In his 1967 study,[8] Milgram set out to establish how well we are connected with each other. He decided on an experiment to determine the 'distance' between two people in the US. He wanted to find out how many steps there would be between two randomly selected people.

To achieve this Milgram wrote to randomly selected people in Wichita and Omaha, asking them to participate in his study. He wanted each of them to send on a package to someone they knew who might be a step closer to two key 'targets' – a housewife in Sharon, Massachusetts, and a stockbroker in Boston.

To do this they would need to follow the carefully outlined instructions:

→ ADD YOUR NAME TO THE ROSTER AT THE BOTTOM OF THIS SHEET, so that the next person who receives this letter will know who it came from.

→ DETACH ONE POSTCARD. FILL IT OUT AND RETURN IT TO HARVARD UNIVERSITY. No stamp is needed. The postcard is very important. It allows us to keep track of the progress of the folder as it moves towards the target person.

→ IF YOU KNOW THE TARGET PERSON ON A PERSONAL BASIS, MAIL THIS FOLDER DIRECTLY TO HIM (HER). Do this only if you have previously met the target person and know each other on a first name basis.

[8] Stanley Milgram, 'The Small World Problem', *Psychology Today*, 1967, Vol 2, 60-67.

→ IF YOU DO NOT KNOW THE TARGET PERSON ON A PERSONAL BASIS, DO NOT TRY TO CONTACT HIM DIRECTLY. INSTEAD, MAIL THIS FOLDER (POSTCARDS AND ALL) TO A PERSONAL ACQUAINTANCE WHO IS MORE LIKELY THAN YOU TO KNOW THE TARGET PERSON. You may send the folder to a friend, relative or acquaintance, but it must be someone you know on a first name basis.

Eventually 42 of the 160 letters made it back, some requiring close to a dozen intermediates. Interestingly, given Karinthy's story nearly 40 years before, the median number of intermediate persons was 5.5.

SIX DEGREES TODAY

It was playwright John Guare who coined the term 'six degrees of separation' in his 1991 play of that title.[9] Of course, Karinthy's story, Milgram's experiment and even Guare's play all existed before the world truly became interconnected through the Internet. With the World Wide Web, social networks and mobile telecommunications, surely we are closer to each other than ever before.

In 2008 a Microsoft survey[10] in the US studied a database of 30 billion text messages sent during June 2006. By looking at the number of common connections in the database, the study suggested that any two people are connected by fewer than seven others.

A number of similar studies in recent years have also suggested that we are no more closely entwined than before the days of digital media. What such media have allowed us though is the capacity both to extend our networks wider and, perhaps more

[9] For more on the play itself, see **http://www.barabasilab.com/ LinkedBook/chapters/3Ch_SixDegreesofSeparation.pdf**, page 29.
[10] **http://www.washingtonpost.com/wp-dyn/content/ article/2008/08/01/AR2008080103718.html**

importantly, to recognise the routes through to our own 'target' more easily.

Through sites like LinkedIn and Facebook, where you can see your contacts' networks, connections have become more visible and more accessible. We will look at this, particularly LinkedIn, in more depth later.

we are no more closely entwined than before the days of digital media

THE SIX DEGREES GAME

At many of my talks and workshops I run a 'Six Degrees Game'. I ask the participants, in groups, to discuss how they would connect with a range of well-known celebrities using their existing contacts.

In the past year alone I've had present at my talks a former teacher at footballer Cristiano Ronaldo's school in Madeira, the former girlfriend to a godson of the Queen, tennis player Andy Murray's next door neighbour and someone whose best friend was decorating Bill Gates' home at that time. I've even had an official lookalike for Bill Gates at one of my talks. Worryingly, though, I didn't recognise him!

Ivan Misner warns that reliance on six degrees of separation is dangerous for people looking to make the most of their network:

> *I believe this myth creates complacency. The notion gives some people a false sense of expectation that connections are bound to happen sooner or later, no matter what they do.*[11]

In *The Tipping Point*, Malcolm Gladwell explains how when Milgram looked at the results of his experiment, he discovered that half of the packages reaching their destination in Sharon, Massachussetts, were delivered by the same three men. Gladwell concluded from this that:

[11] **http://www.entrepreneur.com/marketing/networking/article177986. html**

Six degrees of separation doesn't mean that everyone is linked to everyone else in just six steps. It means that a very small number of people are linked to everyone else in a few steps, and the rest of us are linked to the world through those special few.[12]

Gladwell terms these 'special few' *connectors*. Based on this theory, for six degrees of separation to work effectively for you, you need to have connectors in your network.

When Misner also points out that, based on the results of Milgram's study, only about 29 per cent of the world's population is, in fact, separated from anyone else by around six degrees, you realise that, to get the introductions you need for your business you have to develop a network that offers the right connections, rather than just expect it to happen.

I believe that in the modern, highly networked, economy most of us have the ability to find the connections we need to link us to the people we want to meet. The key is to recognise where those connections are, develop the key relationships and focus our message.

you have to develop a network that offers the right connections

---

IN A NUTSHELL

I believe that in the modern, highly networked, economy most of us have the ability to find the connections we need to link us to the people we want to meet. The key is to recognise where those connections are, develop the key relationships and focus our message.

---

[12] Malcolm Gladwell (2001), *The Tipping Point: How Little Things Can Make A Big Difference*. Abacus.

STRENGTH IN NUMBERS

If you are going to be able to make the most of the six degrees of separation, it is important that you build a network that is strong enough to provide both the routes through to the connections you need and the will to pass on your message.

There is a school of thought that believes that the more people you connect to, the more powerful your network. This school is typified by 'LinkedIn Open Networkers' (who we will look at in more detail in Chapter 15), some of whom count up to 40,000 individuals in their network.

LinkedIn isn't alone. Members of other networks, like Ecademy, Twitter and Facebook, seem to have a strong belief that success is measured purely in numbers, and they drive to build large networks, followers or friends – at the expense of quality interactions.

My approach is somewhat different, as my business's strapline 'Connecting is not Enough' indicates. I believe that your network should be both wide and deep, with a diverse network spreading your reach, but deep relationships with individuals making that reach genuine and worth something. Although I don't believe in connecting for the sake of it, I do believe very strongly that **you need to be connected to a diverse network of people** with different backgrounds, in different industries and from different areas.

In his book *Truth or Delusion*, Misner writes about this:

> *It's simple human nature for people to cluster in groups according to age, education, income, profession, race, neighbourhood, social status, religion and so forth. Hanging out with similar people makes it easier to carry on conversations, share similar experiences, gossip and compare*

notes. It does not tend to expose one to new experiences or new points of view, and it especially does not provide many opportunities to open new frontiers in business or marketing.[13]

From my experience, people whose network mainly consists of people in the same industry as themselves struggle to find the connections they need as easily. If your network is too narrow your contacts will, in all probability, know many of the same people as each other and lack diversity in the people they deal with. Your network also needs to reach a critical mass – a number of people whose reach will enable you to get the referrals you are looking for.

Your network will grow exponentially, but you do need to have a starting point. If, for example, you know 250 people, each of whom knows 250 people, you potentially have a second degree reach of 62,500 people. If each of those second degree contacts knows 250 people, all of a sudden you are, in theory, just two steps away from 15,625,000 people. That's a pretty impressive reach!

If you know 10 people who know 10 people who each know 10 people, your reach is a much more modest 1,000 people.

One coaching client of mine was looking at how he could use his network to develop his career in financial services. He had a low profile role in his firm and was struggling to progress there and so needed to find external mentors to help him drive forward.

I tried to establish his network with him to find the routes it would offer to the people to whom he needed to speak.

[13] Ivan R. Misner, Mike Macedonio and Mike Garrison (2006) *Truth or Delusion? Busting Networking's Biggest Myths*. Thomas Nelson.

'Who do you know through work?' I asked.

'No one,' he replied.

'Well', I asked, 'what are your hobbies?'

'I don't have any.'

'What about your family?'

'We don't really talk to each other!'

So while in much of my writing and speaking I tend to focus on the importance of relationship building rather than network building, there needs to be people in your network with whom to build relationships in the first place. Balance is the key to the issue. Keep your focus on having a network large enough to support your needs but not so big that you can't maintain relationships with the people therein.

FOCUS ON THE CONVERSATION RATHER THAN THE CONNECTION

As you do build your network, take care to make a real connection to people with whom you interact. Some sites now allow you to 'Auto-Connect', simply adding people to your network without ever having a conversation.

take care to make a real connection to people with whom you interact

I am always astounded by the amount of connection requests I receive on LinkedIn and Facebook from people I don't know and who don't even bother to explain why they want to connect with me. If I do connect with them, I'm unlikely to hear from them again. They are no different from people who approach you at networking events, shake your hand, offer you their business card and then walk away. You just become another notch on their networking bedpost!

I fail to understand the value of connecting with someone who doesn't know you or make any attempt to do so. Without any conversation how can there be any trust or any understanding? Why would people without that relationship even buy from you, let alone refer you?

IN A NUTSHELL

I fail to understand the value of connecting with someone who doesn't know you or make any attempt to do so. Without any conversation how can there be any trust or any understanding?

Have a look at your LinkedIn network. If you have connected with people in the past who you didn't know, look at their profiles now. If someone mentioned their name to you, would you know who they were? Would you be willing to refer them to trusted people within your network if they asked? Do you think a connection passed on by you to them would carry any weight?

Maybe it's me but I simply don't understand this 'throw enough mud at the wall and some of it might stick' approach to networking. The larger your network, the harder it becomes to manage. Finding people becomes more difficult and akin to finding a needle in a haystack, however good technology becomes. The job of keeping in touch with people and keeping it personal assumes mighty proportions, while being able to hone in on the right person for a connection becomes increasingly complicated.

At the time of writing, I have a network of around 1,000 people on LinkedIn. I am the first to admit that this is much too high, the result of several years of accepting connection requests indiscriminately before working out the best approach. It is difficult and time consuming for me to look through my network to find the right person, despite the search engine on the site, and I don't know everyone in my network. I would be happier with a network half the size.

While building a wide enough network to offer you diversity of connections, ensure that you build each relationship deep enough to make a difference. As we've already discussed, networking thrives on strong relationships, with trust and understanding being key to people being happy and able to offer you the referrals you need. After all, who refers work to a business card?

You won't be able to build deep relationships with everyone in your network, but attempting to get beyond just the handshake moment is vitally important. I have talked about the six degrees of separation at length, but also be aware of the degrees that exist within your network (see Figure 8.1).

In the centre of your network are the people in whom you trust the most and who trust you in return. They are your champions, the people you will be looking to refer you on an ongoing basis.

ensure that you build each relationship deep enough to make a difference

Figure 8.1 Degrees of your network

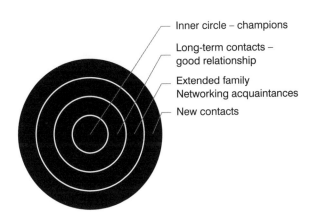

Inner circle – champions

Long-term contacts – good relationship

Extended family
Networking acquaintances

New contacts

Each degree away from the centre are your other connections. Perhaps they are people you haven't seen for a while or people you don't know as well, whose services you haven't experienced or who you have only just met. Many of the people in these outlying areas of your network will be those who are happy to refer you and in a position to do so. It just may be that you are not constantly in the front of their mind or they do not frequently have the opportunity to refer.

It is vital that you stay in touch with people across your network as often as possible and, where possible, in a personal way. Online networks have made it much easier to remain in contact with far more people than ever before, but that personal touch can't be forgotten. Thus, if your network grows too large, keeping in touch becomes increasingly difficult.

THE POWER OF WEAK TIES

In his 1973 paper *The Strength of Weak Ties*,[14] Mark Granovetter of the State University of New York talked about the importance of our acquaintances ('weak ties') in making key connections for us, rather than our close friends ('strong ties').

According to Granovetter's theory, we each are tied into 'clumps' of social structures with our close friends. By their very nature, people within these closely knit clumps will all know each other. By extension, the potential for our close friends to introduce us to someone new is limited.

Our acquaintances, by contrast, are knitted into their own clumps, ones with which we are not as closely associated. According to Granovetter, therefore, our

[14] **http://citeseerx.ist.psu.edu/viewdoc/download?doi=10.1.1.128.77 60&rep=rep1&type=pdf**

relationship with each acquaintance is 'not merely a trivial acquaintance tie but rather a crucial bridge between the two densely knit clumps of close friends'. As he goes on to say, 'these clumps would not, in fact, be connected to one another at all were it not for the existence of weak ties'.

Granovetter concluded that individuals without such weak ties are divorced from 'distant parts of the social system' and deprived of key information from outside their own circle of friends. For Granovetter's study, one of the key ways this would adversely affect an individual was in lack of knowledge of new opportunities in the job market. The key way it could affect you is lack of opportunity to be introduced to potential prospects. Or, in other words, fewer referrals.

it is important that you build a diverse network of acquaintances

It is important, therefore, that you build a diverse network of acquaintances. The more varied the industries, backgrounds and interests reflected in your network, the more 'bridges' you will be building into other networks of people, leading to more opportunities to be referred to the people who need your help. This is where networking groups can be so important in building a strong network of people who can open the right doors for you.

GROWING YOUR NETWORK

If you do recognise that you need to grow your existing network, there are a number of ways to do so. The most obvious is through networking groups, such as local Chambers of Commerce, small business associations, industry events and community groups such as Rotary and Round Table.

When you go to such events with the aim of building your network, remind yourself of that goal. As I discuss in my book ...*and Death Came Third!,* many of us suffer from a fear of meeting new people that drives us into our comfort zone when networking. Often that comfort zone includes spending the whole event speaking with people we already know. Perfectly valid behaviour if you are looking to deepen existing relationships but not when you are looking to meet new people.

You can also look to grow your network through your social contacts. Participate in sports teams, Parent Teacher Associations or get involved in local charities. Get involved in committees to give you even more purpose to meet new people. Join in with friends on social occasions, meeting their acquaintances.

remember that you can connect with people on more than one level

Remember that you can connect with people on more than one level. On a rational level, it is easy to forge a relationship with people with whom you share an interest or, even better, a passion. Whether you share a love of the same sport, are wine connoisseurs, film buffs or travel to similar countries, if you can find something in common with another person, you will find it much easier to connect.

Alternatively, people will connect on a more emotional level. This is something that is much harder to define and is often known as 'chemistry'. Most frequently associated with romantic connections, where you feel that special bond with your partner, we also tend to associate more readily with people with whom we feel comfortable and 'at home'.

Both cases should guide you to the best opportunities for you to connect with the right people. Find those who share the same interests and have the same outlook on life. Just don't restrict yourself to a network with completely the same background, as outlined above.

> **IN A NUTSHELL**
>
> When you meet people at business networking events or in meetings, it can often pay dividends to leave business discussions to one side initially and find out about each other.

When you meet people at business networking events or in meetings, it can often pay dividends to leave business discussions to one side initially and find out about each other. Relax in each other's company and talk about things that matter to you. It will make it much more likely that you will be able to connect on a deeper level and take the relationship to a higher level, where you are both more likely to support each other's business.

NETWORKING FOR LIFE

Many people look at the networking they do now as a short-term project. They are very focused on the immediate goals in their business or their career and are seeking out the people who can help them now. Networking is based on the long-term, though. The most powerful networks are those that have been built over many years and have, therefore, tremendous amounts of trust and understanding ingrained.

I am a member of a networking group called 'The Wild Card Pack'. This network contains some of my closest business colleagues, many of whom I also now count among my closest friends. We network together, often work in collaboration with each other and party together, and many of the referrals to my business come from within this group.

A while ago we noticed that a large proportion of us were the same age, within a couple of years. The power of that struck me immediately. There is no reason why I should not be socialising, working and networking with the same group of people for the next 20 years or more.

We have a tremendous opportunity to build our businesses together and support each other as we grow over a long period of time. Because of the nature of our network and the close relationships between members, as long as that bond isn't broken the potential value of the network to each of our businesses is phenomenal.

the potential value of the network to each of our businesses is phenomenal

In 2009 I was delighted to be invited along to the 10th Anniversary of the Precious Online Awards. The awards celebrate the achievements of women of colour in business and leadership.

Before the presentation of the main award, Precious Entrepreneur of the Year, the 2008 winners Natasha Faith and Semhal Zemikael, who run a semi-precious jewellery business La Diosa, told the audience how the experience had affected them over the previous 12 months.

Both Natasha and Semhal, like many of the women present, are young entrepreneurs in the early stages of their careers. Natasha talked about how supportive other women in the room and in the network had been and about the friends she had made in the year since the last awards ceremony.

What was important, according to Natasha, was that such support and friendship should continue outside the event itself. 'We have an opportunity to grow together and network for life,' she told the audience.

Such long-term thinking about the power of networks is still rare. As networks have matured, we have the opportunity not just to make the connections to help us in our business now, but also to surround ourselves with people who can support us throughout our careers. People with whom we can grow and share our challenges and our achievements, and with whom we have the chance to develop such a bond of trust that the support we can offer each other becomes limitless.

If you haven't done so already, look to your network and recognise those people who are of the same generation and who share the same vision as you. Ask yourself the difference it will make to you if you network with them not just for a year but for many years to come.

REVIEW

This chapter has covered the following:

1 The theory of six degrees of separation.

2 Recognising where your key connections are and how to develop the relationships.

3 Identifying the ideal number and composition for your personal network.

4 Understanding the various levels of your network and the importance of maintaining contact.

5 Ways to grow your network and the power of thinking long term.

Where will your referrals come from?

> 9

→ Opening up your networking groups based
  on their connections to other people

  → The pros and cons of mixing business with pleasure

    → Tracking the right connections

      → Selling through, not to, your network

WHO'S IN YOUR NETWORK?

If you are going to tap into the power of the six degrees of separation, you need to have a clear picture of your network as a whole, and how the people within that network connect with each other.

Most of us have a tendency to pigeonhole people within our network. The way we look at a person is dependent on the relationship we have with them. For example, we are less likely to be aware of what others in our social network do for their profession, or think about the family and social life of our business network.

we interact with people in groups, based on how we know them

We interact with people in groups, based on how we know them. So, sitting in the middle of our network we have our family, friends, social groups, work colleagues, clients and so on (see Figure 9.1).

Figure 9.1   How we pigeonhole our network

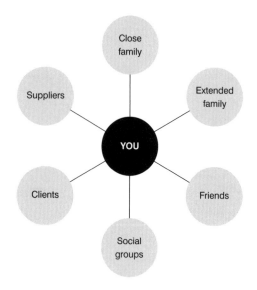

This type of segmentation is fine to an extent, and certainly appropriate in most interactions we have. It does, however, limit the effectiveness of our networking and our ability to reach out to the people to whom we wish to connect. As soon as we pigeonhole people in our network, we begin to write off their relevance to the rest of our network and their ability to help us in different areas.

Last year I was working with a manufacturing company that was struggling to bring in new business. Halfway through the session, as we were looking in more detail at the sales team's networks, the managing director suddenly realised that his wife was in a senior position with a perfect prospective client, yet neither of them had ever made the association!

Another time I was working with a team of business bankers. The deputy regional director went out of the room during a break and came back in to announce that he had just called his brother-in-law and asked for his help. His brother-in-law had given him three referrals on the spot. They had never previously discussed business at all.

I received a referral to the sales director of a major international airline from the same group of bank managers. One of the managers coached a children's football team and the sales director's son played for the team.

> **IN A NUTSHELL**
>
> We see people based on their connection with us –
> and not the connections they have with other people.

The reason such opportunities are often missed is because we write off people's relevance beyond our initial association with them. We see people based on their connection with us – and not the connections they have with other people.

Go to any networking event and you will immediately decide on how useful someone is to you based on their name badge or business card. Who they work with, who their clients may be, who they live next door to or who they play golf with won't come into the equation.

when looking for referrals many of us look only towards the obvious candidates

When looking for referrals many of us look only towards the obvious candidates – our clients and professional introducers. Yet there are so many people who might be equally, or even better placed to refer.

Martine Davies, former alumni programme manager for BDO LLP, an accountancy and business advisory firm, who now holds a similar role at Cranfield University School of Management, believes that one tremendous source of referrals is overlooked by many firms.

One of the most cost-effective and invaluable sources of referrals and potential new business can come from the people who know your firm best – your former employees, your alumni …

When an employee leaves, they take with them the years of learning, development and knowledge that your firm has invested in them. This applies to leavers of all levels – from newly qualified staff to retirees and non-fee earners. If they have had a good experience or if they move on trusting and respecting the firm, they will serve as great brand ambassadors and could become a client or referrer in the future.[15]

What we forget is that the people we know have their own network in just the same way as we do. While you may know someone in their professional capacity, they also have family, friends, their own clients, colleagues and suppliers beyond your relationship (see Figure 9.2).

[15] 'Profit from your alumni network', *Professional Marketing Magazine*, April 2010.

Figure 9.2 A client's network

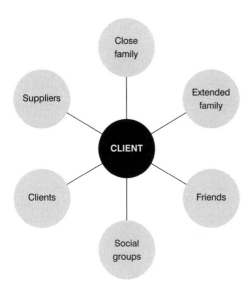

How well do you know what the people in your social network do for a living? List six people closest to you and everything you know about their jobs. What are their job titles? What do their companies do? Who are their clients? What are their roles? What are their challenges?

How about your suppliers or your clients? Who do they deal with when not with you?

Many people struggle to get beyond a job title with some of the closest people in their personal network. Yet once you start this exercise and develop it to understand who they know as a result of what they do, it can be very powerful – particularly when you relate it back to your ideal referral, as discussed in Chapter 6.

KEEPING BUSINESS AND PERSONAL LIVES SEPARATE

It's quite possible that you have an issue with some of the ideas I've covered so far in this chapter. Many people don't like to mix business with pleasure. They like to keep the two separate, as they are concerned that they will be seen to be pushing their business on to people who aren't interested, or they may have very reasonable worries about damaging friendships if an introduction or business deal goes sour.

many people don't like to mix business with pleasure

These are perfectly valid concerns. I certainly wouldn't advocate pushing your business strongly on people who aren't receptive, or manipulating your personal network for business gain. One of the traditional problems with some network marketing companies, for example, is that they encourage their distributors to look to friends and family first. That would be fine if they looked for support, but many just look to their personal networks as their first customers.

When I was 17, one of my close friends invited a group of us over to his house on a summer weekend. This wasn't unusual as his family had a swimming pool, so we'd often go over there. On this occasion, however, we were invited into a small study at the front of the house. A room we had never been in before. At one end of the room stood a flipchart with seats laid out in front of it. I don't think I had ever seen a flipchart before and I wondered what was going on.

As we took our seats, our friend, previously laid back and chilled, launched into a presentation on the wonders of a particular network marketing company. Seeing our friend, a 17-year-old boy, telling us about how great it was to sell domestic product and drawing pyramids on the flipchart, talking about 'downlines' and the 'opportunity' was a little bit disconcerting to say the least.

There had been no prior warning, no invitation. The talk had been sprung upon us. I must admit that it changed my view of my friend and I never quite saw him in the same way again.

So there are dangers to mixing business with personal networks, but only if handled clumsily as in the example above. If you treat your family and friends with respect, avoid pushing business on to them and remain aware of signs of interest or disinterest, you shouldn't burn any bridges.

With the growth of social networks, increased socialising with business networks and more focus on building strong relationships, the line between personal and professional contacts is becoming more blurry. I have met many of my best friends through networking and my Facebook profile means that many of my personal friends and family now understand more about what I do than they ever did before.

> the line between personal and professional contacts is becoming more blurry

However blurry it is, the trick is to recognise where the line lies. Those who feel very uncomfortable mixing business and personal relationships feel happiest drawing a thick line between the two. I understand why, but I always ask them how they would feel if a close family member went bankrupt and lost their house and they could have helped but their relation didn't ask them because of crossing that line. They never feel comfortable at the thought.

The truth is that a line does exist, but it is thinner and more flexible than many people think. If you can help a friend or family member professionally, why wouldn't you? And if they are right for a job, why should your relationship hold them back?

> **IN A NUTSHELL**
>
> If you can help a friend or family member professionally, why wouldn't you? And if they are right for a job, why should your relationship hold them back?

ignoring family and friends as potential referral sources may mean missing out on many opportunities

I was discussing this in a workshop for a client last year and asked who in the room had difficulty with mixing their business and personal networks. One person put her hand up. That person was the head of learning and development, who had booked me for the course on her husband's recommendation!

Ignoring family and friends as potential referral sources, and not recognising the potential of the personal contacts of people across your network, may mean missing out on many opportunities that would make a huge difference to your business.

A study conducted for McKinsey in 2010[16] looked at the different impact of word of mouth on marketing messages when passed on by a friend, family member or other trusted contact, compared to those passed on by strangers. According to the study, 'a high impact recommendation – from a trusted friend conveying a relevant message for example – is up to 50 times more likely to trigger a purchase than is a low-impact recommendation'.

[16] **https://www.mckinseyquarterly.com/A_new_way_to_measure_word-of-mouth_marketing_2567**

TRACKING THE CONNECTIONS YOU NEED

Once you have a clear picture of your network, you will find it much easier to track the connections you need using the six degrees of separation. There are two key ways in which to do this.

1 Prospect to network

Do you have a targeted list of prospects? If so, how do you approach them now? It is quite likely that you cold-call them, or perhaps invite them along to events that may interest them, or try to get yourself invited to events they may already be attending.

How much easier would it be if you knew someone who could connect you to that prospect? Someone who could provide the introduction that guaranteed your call would be put straight through to them and they would listen to what you had to say?

To achieve this you need to know something about that prospect and who they are likely to deal with. If you start to draw a picture of their clients, industry partners and suppliers, you'll hopefully start to recognise people you already know who have their ear.

If it is an individual you want to meet and you know something about their interests then that is even better. If they live locally to you and are a member of a golf club, who do you know who is a member of the same club? Understand the circles in which they mix and ask yourself which mutual contacts you might have as a result. A Google search can often reveal a lot about your prospects.

Once you have developed a picture of your prospect and who they know, start to think about your network. You may not be able to draw the connections out a full six degrees – it will be very difficult to win the introduction if you do – but ask yourself who you might know one or two steps away from the prospect, people who can get you closer to them.

LinkedIn simplifies this process for you. On LinkedIn you can simply type in someone's name as a search and the site will let you know exactly how you are connected. We will cover this in more detail later.

2 Network to prospect

The other approach, and often much easier to complete, is looking at your existing network and understanding who they know.

As discussed above, it is important to get to know your network better. Who do they meet through work? What's their background – where did they used to work? What industry do they know best? On a personal level, what are their interests? What do their closest family do? These may be questions you can only ask of your close network but, if appropriate, be aware of them.

If you understand who you want to meet, it can become quite straightforward to spot connections of value to you. Once again, LinkedIn is there to help you. You can look at their network on LinkedIn and see directly who they know.

SELL THROUGH, NOT TO, YOUR NETWORK

It is very important at this stage to stress that your understanding of your network isn't designed to enable you to sell to them. The reason networking has had such a bad name in the past is because people have seen others in their network as prospects and have acted accordingly.

If you try to sell to people in your network you will very quickly get an unwelcome reputation, and others will not be willing to help or support you, let alone buy from you. Instead of selling *to* your network, you should always keep your focus on selling *through* them, finding the people who want to buy from you with the help of your network.

Let's take networking events as an example. Unless it is a specific 'meet the buyer' event, very few people attend networking events primarily as buyers. In fact, on the contrary, most people there are looking to sell. Taking a step back, surely there can be few worse selling scenarios than a room full of people looking to sell to you! They are not in buying mode, not receptive to your message and, put simply, not interested.

No wonder so many people walk away from networking events complaining that they were a 'waste of time'!

Instead of trying to sell when you attend networking events, try a different approach. I recently met a young woman on the train home from London late in the evening. She was leafing through business cards as the train left the terminus, so I asked her if she had been networking that evening. Unsurprisingly, she had. She was in her first year of work after university and was working for a legal recruitment firm. She had been told by her bosses to attend a number of events but had been given no clear objectives in doing so.

I asked her if she had any business development responsibility within the firm. She didn't. She had no targets to meet, no expectation of bringing in new clients.

This young woman is in a very fortunate position. Without pressure to sell, she can relax when networking and enjoy the experience. Rather than focusing on counter-productive elevator pitches, she can ask questions of other people and engage in genuine conversation.

your understanding of your network isn't designed to enable you to sell to them

By doing so, she will build a network of people who find her engaging, like her and will be happy to help her in the future. When she does reach a position where she is expected to find new business leads, she will be in a very strong position, with a network of people to turn to for introductions and support.

There is no reason why you can't be just as lucky. Take the pressure to sell off yourself when networking and engage in genuine conversation. Talk as much about other people as about you, if not more, and avoid pushing your own product or service.

This is the same approach you should take into all of your networking. Most of the objections people have about discussing business with family and friends stem from a fear of being seen to sell to them, to push their product or services when they are not welcome.

If you aren't doing this but turn to your personal network for help and connections, why should it be resented in the same way – particularly if it is clear that you are equally willing to help them? People only become uncomfortable if they feel targeted in a direct sale, such as when my friend presented the network marketing 'opportunity' to us when we were 17. Most of us are more than happy to help friends and family if we can.

If people in your network want to buy from you, that is different, but it should always be their decision and not forced upon them by you. If you avoid selling, you create the space to allow people to trust you and your business. Once they have that trust and understand your business you can start to look to them as potential champions.

Would you prefer five referrals from one person in your network or one sale?

take the pressure to sell off yourself when networking and engage in genuine conversation

REVIEW

This chapter has covered the following:

1   Guidelines on how to optimise your network's contacts, both personal and business.

2   How you can research the right connections by using LinkedIn.

3   How you can enjoy networking events by not focusing on selling.

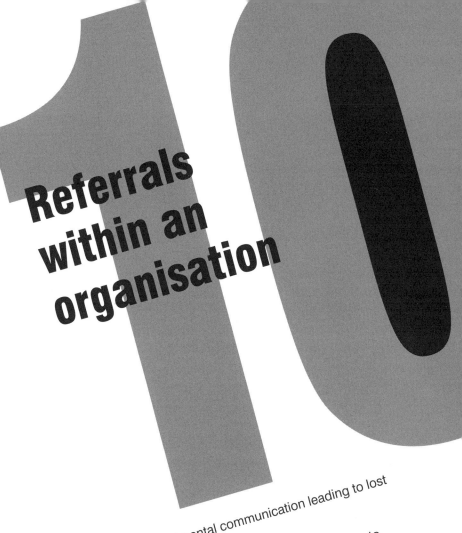

Referrals within an organisation

→ The lack of inter-departmental communication leading to lost referral opportunities

→ Ways of encouraging all levels of staff in your business to recognise opportunities for referral

→ Staff incentives, targets and rewards

I have held my personal account with one major UK high street bank for over 15 years now. My business account is currently with the same bank, but this hasn't always been the case.

Our business used to bank with one of their competitors. Our offices were close to a small town with one main street in which all of the major banks had a branch. Quite often I would go into the main street and visit one or both of the two banks I dealt with. I was familiar to the staff at both.

Occasionally I would be asked by my personal bank to verify my details. One of the questions they would always ask me was to confirm that my occupation was still managing director. They never asked me where my business banked.

The staff in the branch for our business account knew that I would come in to pay in cheques for the business or for other related matters. They never asked me where my personal account was held.

The fact is, hundreds of millions of pounds worth of business must be lost every single year by employees not looking out for opportunities for their colleagues elsewhere in the same company.

> **IN A NUTSHELL**
>
> Hundreds of millions of pounds worth of business must be lost every single year by employees not looking out for opportunities for their colleagues elsewhere in the same company.

Go to a referral-focused networking group and listen to the presentation given by the solicitor present. In most groups of this nature they will have locked out any other solicitors, preventing them from joining as a result of the group's exclusivity policy.

If the member is an employment lawyer, it is highly unlikely that you will hear about litigation, mergers and acquisitions or family law. Week after week the solicitor member will only focus on their own area of speciality. They will not refer to other divisions within their firm.

If, as we have already discussed, trust, understanding and opportunity to refer are the key foundations to enable good quality referrals, where better to start than within your own firm? Yet cross-referring is overlooked by many firms whose staff are more likely to compete than look out for each other.

I am specifically referring to cross-referring rather than simply cross-selling. Often employees are targeted with selling more than one product to a customer, often at the expense of the relationship with that customer. However, recognising a need someone has and referring them to your colleague who may be able to help them specifically with that need is different. You become customer-focused rather than target-driven and the referral is relevant rather than forced.

cross-referring is overlooked by many firms

TRUST AND UNDERSTANDING

Part of the problem lies in the relationships between different parts of the same company. While team-building and meetings may be in vogue, less effort is spent encouraging different sections of the same company to interact. We talk about trust and understanding between people across your network, but how strong are those relationships with people working under the same roof as you?

After I left university I spent four years working in the civil service. The culture within the large departments within which I worked was very much one of silos. Each team worked in a sectioned-off area. When lunchtime came my colleagues would put their work to one

REERRALS WITHIN AN ORGANISATION

side, open up a pack of sandwiches and eat in the same seat in which they'd been working all morning. They would spend all their time not just in the same department but also with the same person with whom they'd worked all day.

I bucked the trend. It's funny to look back at my behaviour considering what I now do for a living. While all of my colleagues remained in their seats during lunch, I would go out with friends from other departments. Although for me it seemed like the normal, sociable thing to do, I was considered quite odd. Yet it was ironic how I would get more support from elsewhere in the office when I needed it!

On Wednesday mornings our offices would open to the public 30 minutes later than normal due to 'staff training'. Traditionally these sessions would see each team in its own silo covering areas of consequence to them. After discussion with my manager, I started visiting other teams and telling them about what we were doing and we invited them to join our meetings to do the same.

In my experience, too little of this happens in business now. Teams are kept apart from each other with people generally socialising with others within their own department. Even in smaller businesses where people from across the company sit close together and are more likely to socialise with each other, it's not common for people to discuss their jobs and goals.

IN A NUTSHELL

Companies that focus on building connections between different parts of the business and educating their staff in more than just their own job will be able to tap into a wealth of opportunities.

Some companies do use cross-selling charts. Salespeople are armed with grids displaying details of their clients and all the services they offer, enabling them to ensure that they raise every opportunity to sell to that client. After all, we are often told that it is six times more expensive to recruit a new customer than to sell more to an existing one.

But if salespeople are not rewarded when they support other parts of the business, and as a result don't have relationships with individuals in those departments, such charts will only be an afterthought.

Social events within the firm offer great opportunities to mix. Working with a property development company I asked the participants on my workshop to list the networks to which they belonged. A number of them had the company's sports and social club at the top of their list.

social events within the firm are great opportunities to mix

Internal networking events, such as women's networks, also offer great opportunities for staff to mix and learn about each other. If you have the opportunity, go to these events and make sure you speak to people from other parts of the business, rather than just those you know. Find out about their role, their challenges and who they deal with.

Most importantly, find out if there are opportunities for you to learn from each other, share experiences and work on the same projects, and whether you are targeting similar clients.

Communal areas such as the staff canteen also offer the opportunity to build your internal network. If you are in the habit of finding the empty table and eating on your own, or sitting with your colleagues all the time, break that habit and ask others if you can join them. Get to know other people in your own firm and find out how you can help them achieve their goals.

THE TROUBLE WITH TARGETS

The next step forward from building relationships across silos within an organisation is to incentivise everyone to look for new business opportunities, not just the sales team and not just people working on a particular product or service.

incentivise everyone to look for new business opportunities

Keeping targets and rewards dependent on just one area of work restricts the likelihood of people seeking referrals for other parts of the business. If companies recognise and reward efforts to create connections irrespective of who makes the sale, they will start to see more new business being generated through the efforts of staff across the business.

In many businesses the roles of new business generation and account management are separated. The person who deals with the client on a day-to-day basis and who is best placed to ask for referrals has no responsibility and receives no reward for asking for those referrals. Meanwhile, the person who does have the focus and stands to benefit has no further influence with that client.

This is surely one of the main reasons why so few referrals come in from clients.

Put simply, personal goals lead to selfish behaviour and restrict the flow of referrals internally. This problem gets reinforced in times of economic turbulence, as people become more concerned with protecting their own job and meeting their own targets, perhaps at the expense of the firm's wider interests.

> **IN A NUTSHELL**
>
> Personal goals lead to selfish behaviour and restrict the flow of referrals internally.

Personal targets and rewards also reinforce narrow 'tunnel' thinking, with people solely focused on their own sale and own bonuses.

Companies need to break out of this narrow thinking and inspire their staff to refer each other. Bonuses and commissions should be in place for introductions to other departments, with a share offered in business won to everyone involved, whatever their job description.

It's not just the sales team who should be included. PAs, receptionists and customer service representatives all have jobs where they deal with the company's clients and suppliers. Everyone who works there has their own personal network.

Whenever I work on a referrals strategy with companies, I try to encourage them to send staff from across the business on workshops, not just the people targeting new business. In one case the financial director came on a workshop. He had never passed a referral over to the sales team before that session. In the next two months he passed seven.

Cross-sales and cross-referrals need to be taken seriously and encouraged in any referral strategy. Without it, companies are just throwing money away.

REVIEW

This chapter has covered the following:

1 Developing techniques to generate more business by cross-referring.

2 Recognising areas where you and your colleagues can focus to generate more referrals.

REERRALS WITHIN AN ORGANISATION

How to select the right networks for you

- → Different types of networking group and how to recognise the networks that fit your *primary* goals
- → The range of online networks targeting different goals
- → The importance of return on investment – your networking budget
- → The referral mix
- → What success looks like and the importance of commitment
- → Time to leave

In Chapter 2 we talked about the networking myth – the fact that networking groups in themselves don't produce referrals. Formal networks can, however, play a part in your referrals strategy, particularly if you need to grow your network to extend your reach.

In this chapter we will take a broader look at networking groups and how to select the right one for you. This is a key business skill to get right if you want to avoid wasting both time and money in the wrong place, or interacting in the wrong way.

Think back to the most recent networks you have attended. Why did you originally go to that specific event? In some cases you will have done your research and identified the right group for you, but it is more likely that you responded to an invitation, either from someone in your network or direct from the organisers.

If you were invited along by a membership group, someone may have asked you to join. Depending on the nature of the network this may have been a strong sales pitch or a gentle invitation.

Many regular groups, where the focus is on building membership, will hold 'visitor days'. The aim is to pack the room with people and create a buzz, which will make people want to join. Unfortunately, this leads to people joining groups for the wrong reasons – because they like the buzz and anticipate some business being done. Without setting clear objectives for their own membership they often stay in the group for only a few months before walking away disillusioned.

This is why some networking groups get a bad name even though the principle and the agenda are strong. When people join without clear goals or an understanding of what they want from membership they set a pattern of behaviour, which others will copy.

Bad habits breed bad habits (turning up sporadically, not preparing, failure to follow up) and a lack of focus becomes contagious. Many groups

bad habits breed bad habits and a lack of focus becomes contagious

simply turn into social clubs precisely because of a group lack of focus.

CLASSIFICATION OF NETWORKING GROUPS

To select the right networking event for you, you have to focus on the *primary influences* – your business or personal goals. While many people classify networks by the time of day they meet or make-up of their membership, I prefer to start from what they can achieve for you.

> **IN A NUTSHELL**
> Broadly speaking, business networks can achieve one of three primary goals for each member.

Broadly speaking, business networks can achieve one of three primary goals for each member. They can be:

→   profile building;

→   brain building; or

→   referral building.

Profile building

For many people the key goal of networking is to become better known, either as a business or personally. This is particularly important if you have recently started a new business, moved into a new area or launched a new product.

I'm sure you've heard the phrase 'it's not what you know, it's who you know'. You now need to take that to another level. If you want to build your profile effectively, it's more important to focus on who knows you and what they say about you.

> **IN A NUTSHELL**
>
> If you want to build your profile effectively, it's more important to focus on who knows you and what they say about you.

It's important, therefore, to be aware of where you want to build your profile when looking for the right networks to help you do so. If it's in a particular area or industry, you should be seeking out networks in those areas. Similarly, if you want to become better known among a certain group of businesspeople, network where they will be present.

you need to have a clear idea of what you want to be known for

I am a member of a private members' club in London where many leading entrepreneurs often hold meetings. By being seen in the club on a regular basis I meet a lot of those entrepreneurs and they are reminded of my presence.

When you network to become better known you need to have a clear idea of what you want to be known for, and how you will communicate that through your network. It's one thing for fellow members of my club to know who I am but that doesn't hold much value for me if they don't understand what I do or who I do it for.

Profile-building networks tend to meet less frequently than some, often monthly or even quarterly, but with larger numbers. This gives you the opportunity to meet new people each time you attend, while also having the opportunity to touch base with people you've met at previous events.

To be effective, you will need to commit on a regular basis so that you are frequently seen and people start to show an interest in you. Your profile won't rise simply by attending one event; you need to be seen again and again.

Brain building

Many networking events offer you the opportunity to hear guest speakers, meet with people from across your industry or ask your peers for support. These are the networks where you can focus on your self-development goals, which I term 'brain building'.

You can use your networks to learn new things and give your business new ideas and a fresh perspective. If you understand what your goals are from networking, you can then pick the right groups to give you this perspective.

If your understanding of your own business and industry are key, look to industry associations and see the range of events they put on. Where you see guest speakers billed, work out how they might help with challenges in your business at the moment and what you want to take away from these meetings.

So many audiences walk away with little because they have come to be entertained rather than learn. Set yourself some clear goals from hearing a speaker and understand what you will look to implement after the talk.

I'm a member of the Professional Speaking Association. Over the last eight years my membership of the Association has given me the opportunity to develop my craft and business by learning from some of the leading lights in the field, both from the UK and internationally. I have also developed a network of peers to whom I can turn for advice at any time and have a co-mentoring relationship with a fellow member.

I am also a member of a mastermind group of business peers that meets on a regular basis to share our challenges and provide ideas, feedback

set yourself some clear goals from hearing a speaker

and support. Membership of one such group helped to turn my business around two years ago when I was involved in an unsuccessful project. My fellow members helped me to realise the project could never succeed because my heart wasn't in it.

Referral building

If you are planning to attend networking events or join networking groups as part of your referrals strategy, you need to think about how each one of these could help. Consider the key foundations of referral success that we have already discussed:

→ The importance of trust

→ The building of relationships

→ Ensuring that other people understand your business

→ Ensuring that your contacts have the ability to refer you

→ Ensuring that you have opportunities to refer.

Now ask yourself, how will each network help you deliver one or more of those elements?

Organisations like the global networking group Business Network International (BNI) are designed to deliver one or more of these elements through the size of group, frequency of meeting and format. They don't invite guest speakers – it's all about the members building trust in each other and understanding each other's business.

If you want to network to generate referrals, I wouldn't recommend taking half-measures. You need to understand the commitment you are willing and able to make, look at which groups fit that level of commitment and ask whether you can get the results you are looking for if you join.

It may be that you join a group that meets less frequently but then set aside time outside these events to meet with fellow members regularly. Whichever path you choose, if you want referrals, you need to build trust and understanding with people who have the opportunity to refer you.

> **IN A NUTSHELL**
>
> Whichever path you choose, if you want referrals, you need to build trust and understanding with people who have the opportunity to refer you.

NETWORKING ONLINE

The growth of social networking, or online networks, in recent years has added further opportunities, or confusion, to the networking scene. With so many invitations to different online networks being sent every day, many people struggle to know which ones to join and engage in.

use exactly the same approach to networks online as for face-to-face networks

It doesn't have to be too complicated. My advice is to use exactly the same approach to networks online as we have discussed for face-to-face networks. Understand what you want to achieve through membership, look at what they achieve based on the classifications above and recognise the commitment you need to put in if you do join.

It is perfectly possible that each online network could be used for a different goal or set of goals. It may well be that people use the same network for different reasons from each other, but if you have a clear goal and understand how to use each network to that end, you will see more benefits from membership.

Profile building

On both Facebook and LinkedIn I have groups to
post discussions, blogs and interesting links and
hopefully attract more people's interest in what I do.
Whenever a member of either page comments on a
post, their network sees that activity and becomes
aware of my work.

Ecademy and Xing are among many social networks
with a strong membership of smaller businesses. By
blogging and contributing in forum discussions on those
networks I can raise my profile among the membership.

I regularly post networking tips and blogs on Twitter.
If people who follow my tweets find them interesting,
they may retweet them (copy them) to their followers,
thereby raising my profile with a new group of people.

Brain building

Both Twitter and LinkedIn can be used for market
research and to get feedback on new ideas. LinkedIn
has a very active questions and answers section, as
well as groups for almost any business interest and
in-depth information on many companies who have
profiles on the site.

On Twitter you can ask questions of the people
following you (it's often more tempting now to ask
something on Twitter rather than searching on Google)
and track any posts of interest by searching for key
words and topics. Additionally, many experts, such as
MediaCoach's Alan Stevens, hold open surgeries on
Twitter where they will answer any questions on their
topic of expertise.

Referral building

We are going to look at LinkedIn as a referral tool in
Chapter 15. Although it can be used for both profile
and brain building, as outlined above, for me LinkedIn's
main power is as a referral tool. It is built around

people's networks and giving you the opportunity to find the connections you need and ask your network to introduce you.

In addition, you can build your referral network through the connections you build online. While Ecademy is, for me, primarily a profile-building tool, fellow members of the BlackStar level of Ecademy membership have become the most productive source of champions for my business. In fact, it's a small group within BlackStar who regularly champion me. As well as referring me, they provide my support network, as the two often overlap (trust and understanding being equally important in a peer support group).

you can build your referral network through the connections you build online

While the network is brought together through an online platform, most of the relationship building is done face to face. In fact I rarely use Ecademy online these days, with my profile-building activity focused elsewhere. Ecademy provides the tools and the opportunity, and the relationship building is then down to the individuals in the group.

Such a targeted use of social networks delivers better results than the mass approach favoured by many. While I have profiles on many social networks, I use only a handful proactively, keeping me much more focused on the results I am looking for and able to handle the time commitment more effectively.

Look individually at each network, your goals from membership and actions needed. As the necessary functionality has become more widely available, there has been a growth in the number of people setting up standard profiles across online networks and taking their 'feed' on one (especially Twitter) and then posting it automatically elsewhere. In addition, many people automatically connect with exactly the same people on every platform they join.

I can't understand the point of replicating the same information to the same people in different places. If you join more than one online network, you should have different connections, post different content, be there for a different purpose or a combination of all three. Anything else simply isn't an efficient use of your time or effort.

What you should look to do is establish the *primary* reason you want to network and then find out which networks are best suited to those goals (see Table 11.1). If you can then achieve other results from your participation in those networks, that is great. But get your primary goal right first.

Table 11.1   Setting objectives from networks

NAME OF NETWORK	PRIMARY GOAL	SECONDARY GOAL

GETTING RESULTS FROM YOUR MEMBERSHIP

Once you have decided which networks to attend to generate referrals for your business, you then have to be more specific in setting your expectations of success. Setting clear goals makes a tremendous difference to how well networking groups work for you as a referral-generation tool, and such goals are important in both forecasting and measuring how effective your strategy is.

If you want fellow members of your networking group to refer business to you, it makes sense for you to understand what you want to receive before you set out. Be clear about what success looks like. If you fail to do so, you will find it harder to achieve and won't recognise it if it does come along.

be clear about what success looks like

Word reached me once of a member who left one of our networking groups, citing its failure to produce enough new business as a reason. In fact, he called his year of membership 'a waste of time'. The member in question was a local business manager for a major retail bank. In the previous 12 months with his local group he had converted six new customers (or 'switchers') from referrals received from the group.

Over the subsequent years I have asked a number of bank managers, from peers at the same bank to senior management both there and elsewhere, to help me to understand this. I ask them how many switchers they would have needed to justify their membership. Without exception they have told me that three new business accounts would have sufficed.

The bank manager in question had, in fact, doubled what a cross-industry consensus agreed was a reasonable return on his investment. But he had walked away decrying it as 'a waste of time'. To me there can only be one explanation for this – he didn't know what success would look like; he hadn't set any goals.

Instead of celebrating each converted referral as a step towards his targets, he had walked away in the weeks that he hadn't received a referral feeling frustrated. Understanding what return on investment you are targeting ensures that you can keep on track, change your approach if it's not working and celebrate success when it comes along.

A REASONABLE RETURN

When setting goals for a return on your networking, ensure that you set them at the right level. Too many people join networking groups either without setting any goals at all or just looking to earn back their membership fee. If you join a group explicitly to generate referrals, that should be reflected in your vision of success.

To work out your return on networking, you need to factor in the following:

→ Cost of membership

→ Cost of meetings

→ Cost of your time

→ Travel time and cost

→ Opportunity cost (what alternative marketing activity could you undertake in the time spent networking, and what return would you expect that to produce?)

→ Time and cost of meeting fellow members outside the meetings and follow-up activity.

Immediately you should be able to see that a sufficient reward for networking membership is substantially more than just your money back. This is a good thing to know, because it will drive your activity within the group. If you know that you have set a higher target for your return, you will begin to ask for the right business.

Too many people go to networking events and aim for the 'low-hanging fruit', simply trying to sell to the people in the room and pitching at a level they feel is appropriate. As a result, they miss out on a host of opportunities potentially available to them.

I worked with one group in Oxford and asked the members who among them had set a financial goal from their membership. One of the members was a business coach and she was targeting a return of £30,000 per year from the group. That sounds like a reasonable return for a business coach from one networking group.

I asked her the value of a minimum sale for her and it was just a few pounds – I think she had some books and CDs for sale. I then asked her the value to her business of her ideal referral.

a sufficient reward for networking membership is more than just your money back

'£200,000,' she replied.

'What would a £200,000 referral look like?' I asked.

'A board of directors where I coach every board member once a month for a year.'

Would it be an unreasonable goal for a good business coach who is respected and trusted by her fellow members to secure one contract of that nature from a networking group with 30 members? That's one converted referral from around 50 meetings with 29 other people. One from 1,450 opportunities.

If she had planned to ask for exactly that referral then it probably wouldn't be too big an expectation. But she wasn't. Because she was only targeting a return of £30,000, the 'dream referral' outlined above wasn't on her radar. She wasn't asking for it; fellow members didn't know to look for the opportunity.

IN A NUTSHELL

Ignore the low-hanging fruit and start asking for the referrals that will secure the best possible return on investment. Remember the six degrees of separation and tap into the connections of the other group members, rather than trying to sell to them.

Ignore the low-hanging fruit and start asking for the referrals that will secure the best possible return on investment. Remember the six degrees of separation and tap into the connections of the other group members, rather than trying to sell to them.

If you are struggling to identify your ideal return on networking, look at the forecasts you have set for your business this year. How much revenue are you targeting? How much needs to come from networking activity, and how much will you get from outside networking groups? The balance should guide your response.

THE REFERRAL MIX

Once you have set your return from networking, the temptation will be to break it down into monthly or quarterly targets. But networking doesn't work like this. Not all referrals are equal, as we are about to discuss, so returns don't fit neatly into calendar-based chunks. In addition, the number and quality of referrals you generate should grow the more you develop the relationships with fellow members, so the returns in month 12 should be substantially more than those in month 1.

> **IN A NUTSHELL**
>
> Not all referrals are equal, so returns don't fit neatly into calendar-based chunks.

You need to have a different way to set targets. And this should reflect the range of business you are looking for.

In reality, the business coach in the example above, like any member of a networking group, won't be asking for the same dream referral every week. A large number of us will be looking for a range of clients buying different products or services at different price levels. That is healthy for your business. Your referral network should reflect this.

Besides, fellow members will soon switch off if you ask for the same referrals from every meeting. By mixing your requests you are also keeping them engaged and developing their understanding of your business meeting by meeting.

fellow members will soon switch off if you ask for the same referrals from every meeting

I asked the business coach for the minimum level of business she would look for and her dream referral. There are a range of opportunities in between and your return from your networking group will often reflect this.

Create your referral mix – the range of business that you target to reach your financial goal. For example, a web designer may look for £120,000 return from their networking in a year. Rather than target £10,000 per month, they create a referral mix, made up of bread and butter referrals that keep the business ticking along, steak and chips referrals that are that bit more satisfying and the dream referral, or caviar, that comes along rarely but lifts the business to another level (see Figure 11.1 overleaf).

Figure 11.1 The referral mix (a)

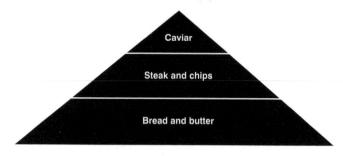

In the case of our web designer, that may break up into a mix of simple brochure sites (bread and butter referrals), more complicated e-commerce sites (steak and chips) and the dream, caviar referral of a social networking site with a range of functionality. Now the web designer can look to how many of each of the products they would need to meet their targets. Their mix might look something like that in Figure 11.2.

Figure 11.2 The referral mix (b)

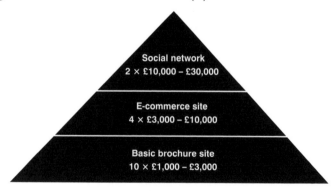

Once you have your referral mix in place, it becomes easy to track what is working and adapt what you ask for. Receiving too many bread and butter referrals? Change what you are asking for. Not getting enough steak and chips referrals? Change the way you are asking. Not getting close to that caviar moment? Are you asking for it enough?

As you judge the flow of referrals you may also change your mix, realising that the caviar referrals are easier to gain than you thought, or that you can cope with more steak and chips referrals.

Be aware of your conversion rates though. The figures in Figure 11.2 reflect *converted* referrals. If you need to receive three referrals to secure a piece of business, you'd need to reflect that in your referral mix. Also bear in mind that conversion rates will often be much better for basic business than for your dream referral.

HOW YOUR REFERRAL MIX FEEDS YOUR MESSAGE

Many people who attend regular referral-focused networking groups struggle with what to say during their presentation every week. As already discussed, in many groups it becomes apparent that little preparation or thought has gone in to what people present and they end up saying the same thing week in, week out, to little or no effect.

> the referral mix leads to more targeted messages

Once you have your referral mix in place, that problem is solved. Each meeting you can simply ask for one of the referrals in your mix. Our web designer, for example, may look one week for a referral for an e-commerce site. They can use their presentation to paint a picture of someone who may need an e-commerce site, perhaps a small retailer, and ask for connections to similar businesses.

In this way, the referral mix leads to more targeted messages. And it is those messages that will make it easier for people in the group to refer you.

A few years ago I met Tony Westwood. Tony is a golfing coach who has developed a very different approach to teaching his students. Whereas most golf pros will focus on a golfer's stance, grip and swing, Tony, an NLP (neuro-linguistic programming) practitioner, gets his students to focus on the ball, where they want it to go and where they need to hit it to get that result.

When I met Tony he was a member of a referral-focused networking group close to home. He mainly received referrals for individual golf lessons and the occasional corporate golf day from a group. But that wasn't what he was really looking for. Tony was looking to develop a number of presentations around his unique approach to golf coaching and also to work closely with much smaller groups at corporate days. The problem was that he wasn't asking for those referrals.

It turned out that Tony's approach to coaching golf didn't really differ from the approach he should have been taking with his referral group. 'Think of the group as the ball and the green as where you want that ball to go.'

As Tony explained, in golf, if you hit the ball on the right-hand side it will travel to the left; if you hit the ball on the left-hand side it will travel to the right; and if you hit it in the middle . . . you get the idea!

Where you 'hit' your networking group will determine what it can do for you. If you ask for one thing, that is what you'll get. If you ask for something else, then that is what you'll get.

So, when you are networking it is important that you picture where you want your group to take you. Aim for the green, not just a hundred yards down the fairway, and then work out how you will need to hit the ball to get there. Think about how your presentations and requests will help you to achieve your goals.

Following our meeting, Tony changed his approach, to make it more in tune with his approach to golf. He's now the head professional at Clube Nacional de Golfe in Portugal.

where you 'hit' your networking group will determine what it can do for you

'I guess you could say my approach worked as I would not have found my current position here in Portugal without more of a "laser-like" focus to my networking,' Tony said recently. 'Your help allowed me to look at what I was doing and where I would like to be working and bringing up my family.'

> **IN A NUTSHELL**
>
> Your referral mix feeds your results. It guides you towards your goal by reminding you of what you are looking for and then helping you decide the best request to make to gain the referrals you are targeting.

Your referral mix feeds your results. Rather than just hitting the ball (turning up and giving an unprepared presentation), it guides you towards your goal by reminding you of what you are looking for and then helping you decide the best request to make to gain the referrals you are targeting.

YOU NEED TO COMMIT

Whatever else you do, if you decide to join a networking group to generate referrals, give it time to work and don't enter into it in a half-hearted manner. You have to commit if you're going to succeed. We've already talked at length about the importance of building trust and understanding with your potential champions. These groups are designed to do just that, but you have to be present to make it happen.

Besides, who will refer you to their key contacts if you show a lack of commitment in the way you interact with them and with the group? This is your audition;

people will judge you on the professionalism and reliability you display as a member of the group.

There are some effortless things you can do within a referral network that will build your reputation and positive profile among fellow members. These include being at the meetings early and leaving last; preparing in advance and following up referrals you have both promised and received.

Apart from demonstrating that you are a good person to network with, it's in your interest to do this. While many members arrive just in time for a meeting to begin and leave as soon as the formal business has concluded, more in-depth conversations tend to take place once the meeting has ended, when the atmosphere is more relaxed and less hurried. I have seen so much business done at this time among a handful of people who stay around to talk.

As I have mentioned earlier, it's also important to set up regular one-to-one or small group meetings with fellow members. You need to build a deep understanding of your business among your group if you hope to receive quality referrals, and you can't build that from simply delivering thirty 60-second presentations each week.

GIVERS GAIN

One thing that you will also frequently hear people talk about at referral networks is the concept of Givers Gain®, coined by BNI founder Ivan Misner. Put simply, Givers Gain is another way of stating the familiar concept of giving to receive and 'what goes around comes around'.

As I have often pointed out to groups, if everyone turns up just looking to be given referrals, where are they going to come from? If everyone looks to pass them out, someone has to be the recipient. It's in everyone's interest to ensure that referrals are passed to keep the group worthwhile for all.

Misner has said that this law is 'based on the social capital theory of the law of reciprocity. It's not a transactional law, it's a transformational law. I help you and you help me and we both do better as a result.'

WHEN SHOULD YOU LEAVE A NETWORKING GROUP?

With a wide array of choices of networking group available, it can be very tempting either to 'play the field' and visit many groups rather than commit to one, or to leave a group after a period of time for a change of scene.

Remember that relationships take a while to grow, so be careful not to cancel your membership in frustration just as people are close to being ready to refer you. Take on board the other advice in this book about growing relationships with your champions and you should be in a better position to judge how effective the group might be for you in the future.

Equally, some groups do take a while to get off the ground and many of them have a fluctuating life cycle, with new blood needed on a regular basis to strip away complacency and prevent them simply becoming social clubs. If fellow members are turning up when they choose and going through the motions, you need to see whether there is a core of members who want to change the culture. If not, it might be time to move on.

Some people leave groups because they feel they have outgrown them, need a change or now have the relationships and will continue to get referrals from fellow members without turning up. Before you do so, be sure you are making the right decision.

> relationships take a while to grow, so be careful not to cancel your membership in frustration

out of sight
could lead to
you becoming
out of mind

If you are receiving a regular stream of referrals, don't take it for granted that it will continue if you leave. You may have strong relationships with fellow members because you see them regularly at meetings. Out of sight could lead to you becoming out of mind, particularly if a competitor joins in your place.

> **IN A NUTSHELL**
>
> If you are receiving a regular stream of referrals from a networking group, don't take it for granted that it will continue if you leave.

If you are in need of a change and your business employs staff, or you have business partners, rather than leave someone else could take your place in the group. You can then still turn up occasionally, keeping the relationships you have personally developed running and still maintaining the benefit of long-term commitment to the group.

I would certainly advise anyone thinking of leaving because they have 'outgrown the group' to think twice, and certainly not publicise the fact. One person in my network did precisely this, telling all and sundry that his business was now too big to associate with members of the group he had been part of for over five years. Needless to say, he managed to destroy his relationships and reputation in one fell swoop because of his arrogance.

Dave Clarke, CEO of UK business network NRG, spoke to me about the reasons people quit.

'Many people leave groups because they never really worked out why they should be there in the first place. Then there are the people who do it for a year and stop because they think it isn't working. The great shame is that they are usually at the point where their investment is about to reap rewards,' he explained.

'They have become known, liked, rated and trusted. Instead of strengthening the relationships they have built they move on to start the whole process again with new people.

'Most weeks I will be at an event and someone will ask where X or Y is because they have something for them. If I say they have left the group they almost always ask for a recommendation to somebody else, even if I offer to pass their message on.'

Most groups will not suit you for ever and there will be a time to move on. The important thing is to make sure you do so in a positive way and for the right reasons, without burning your bridges. It would be a shame if you were to destroy months or years of relationship building and unnecessarily discard the social capital you have built up.

REVIEW

This chapter has covered the following:

1 Identifying different types of networking group and their benefits.

2 Why some networkers fail and the dangers of pre-conception.

3 Knowing your *primary* networking goals and identifying the face-to-face and online networks that best serve those goals.

4 Targeting your networking with different goals and making the most efficient use of your time and effort.

5 Recognising success and getting the best possible return on your networking investment.

6 Using a targeted referral mix to maximise effectiveness.

7 Understanding how to commit, give in order to receive and when to leave.

HOW TO SELECT THE RIGHT NETWORKS FOR YOU

part 4

How to get your network to refer you

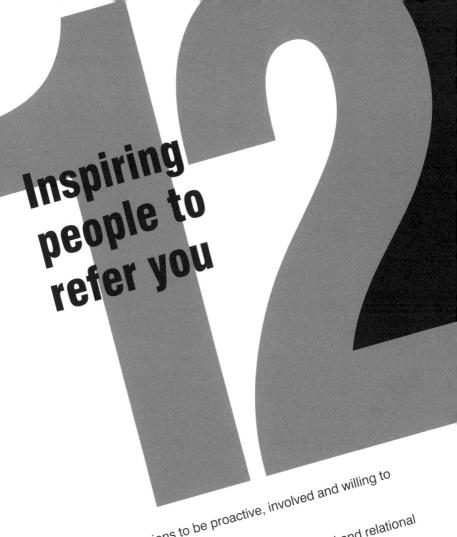

Inspiring people to refer you

→ Helping your champions to be proactive, involved and willing to refer again and again

→ The advantages and disadvantages of transactional and relational approaches to referral generation

→ Referring as a positive experience

→ The importance of asking for support

We may well be surrounded by people who would be happy to refer us, by people who have the opportunity to do so and by people who have the necessary understanding to refer us. Yet something is still missing. If it weren't, businesses would be buzzing with received referrals and you wouldn't be reading this book.

How can you shift your network from a position where they'd be happy and able to refer but don't, to one where they are referring you on a regular basis?

if no one asks, nothing happens

I would hazard a pretty reasonable guess that the main barrier to regular referrals at the moment is that everyone involved, including you, is reactive and passive about generating opportunities, rather than proactive. A champion will refer you if someone else in their network asks them to recommend a service provider and you fit the bill. If no one asks, nothing happens; they are not thinking about opportunities or actively looking for them.

Similarly, you will gratefully accept referrals offered and may take some small moves towards proactively asking for them, using some of the techniques highlighted earlier in this book, but the approach is general rather than focused on individual champions.

Let's change that. A successful referrals strategy treats everyone in your network as an individual and seeks to make it as easy and as likely as possible for each of those individuals to refer you. The first place to start is recognising what will inspire them to do so.

IN A NUTSHELL

A successful referrals strategy treats everyone in your network as an individual and seeks to make it as easy and as likely as possible for each of those individuals to refer you.

WHO DO *YOU* REFER?

Many companies rely on financial incentives and rewards to inspire people to refer them. We will look at this in more detail later in the chapter, but before understanding how effective that approach is for others, let's look at how effective it is for *you*.

Take a piece of paper and write down the names of five people or companies you have referred recently (see Table 12.1 overleaf). In particular, think of the most valuable referrals you have passed and also people you have referred most frequently.

→ Why did you pass the referrals?

→ What inspired you to do so?

→ Did they ask you for the referrals or did you simply volunteer them?

→ Was it a 'passive referral' – in other words, did you respond to a request for a recommendation? Or was it a 'proactive referral' where you spotted an opportunity and created the connection?

Alongside each name score out of 10 how well you trust that person or business, how well you understand what they do and the opportunity you have to refer them. Write down the key factors that motivated you to refer them.

Look back at your list and try to see if there are any common factors that motivated you to refer. Are you only referring people in whom you have strong levels of trust? What difference does it make to you how well you understand their business or whether you are speaking to the right people on a regular basis? Are you motivated by financial reward or something more esoteric?

Table 12.1 Businesses or people you already refer

COMPANY/ PERSON YOU REFERRED	NUMBER/VALUE OF REFERRALS PASSED	TRUST, UNDERSTANDING, OPPORTUNITY	WHAT MOTIVATED YOU TO REFER?

Now look back at the list of people you referred. Did you know someone else who could have done an equally effective job? If so, were there particular factors that meant you referred them at the expense of someone else?

As well as understanding what inspired you to refer, did the person you referred make it easy for you? What was in place that made it straightforward for you to refer?

Now I'd like you to create two more lists. Write down the names of three people or businesses you'd love to refer but don't (see Table 12.2) and also three you simply wouldn't be willing to refer (see Table 12.3).

In the case of those you'd like to refer, what's stopping you? Do you like them personally but don't have enough of a grip on their business to make the referral? Perhaps you don't understand who their customers are or how to make the introduction.

If you were to take steps to refer them, what needs to happen? What can they do to make it easier for you to refer them? If you took on the task of making at least one effective referral for them, what would you need to do?

Table 12.2 Businesses or people you'd like to refer

COMPANY/PERSON YOU WOULD LIKE TO REFER	TRUST, UNDERSTANDING, OPPORTUNITY	WHAT NEEDS TO HAPPEN FOR YOU TO REFER?

Now look at the list of people or businesses you're not willing to refer. Why not? Is it simply a matter of a lack of trust or poor personal chemistry? Or has your experience of their services been a negative one?

If that person or company had to rely on referrals from you in order to save their business, what steps would they have to take to change your mind? How would you expect them to turn the situation around and make you their champion? No cheating allowed by saying 'they couldn't'! They *have* to make you their champion to save their business – what could they do to make that happen?

Table 12.3 Businesses or people you wouldn't refer

COMPANY/PERSON YOU WOULDN'T REFER	TRUST, UNDERSTANDING, OPPORTUNITY	WHAT NEEDS TO HAPPEN FOR YOU TO REFER?

If you bring your lists together you should now have a record of ways people can inspire you to refer them. Some of those approaches may be very *transactional*, such as commissions for referrals received, the understanding of referrals back to you in return or being taken out as a thank you. Others may be more *relational* – simply because you like them and want them to succeed, for example.

These are the approaches that work for you and can give you some insight into different approaches you can take to inspire others. However, not everyone is the same. Whether people are more inspired by transactional or relational interactions very much depends on their personality type. We'll look at both these types of interaction in turn.

TRANSACTIONAL INSPIRATIONS

I talked in Chapter 4 about the popularity of *incentive schemes*, such as the ones operated by the Sunday Times Wine Club and health clubs to incentivise existing members to introduce new members.
In addition to the drawbacks I mentioned earlier, when the negative impact of being associated with a substandard product or service outweighs the attraction of the incentive reward, in my experience most of these incentive schemes tend to have minimal impact, particularly as people move on to other things and forget about the incentive.

Sinclair Beecham, co-founder of Pret à Manger, shared his experience at an event I attended last year. Inviting questions from the audience throughout his presentation, Sinclair was asked by one self-confessed 'loyal customer' why, unlike many of their competitors, they didn't operate a loyalty scheme.

'I hate loyalty schemes. Why not just work your butt off and do extra for your customer?' responded Sinclair.

The person who originally asked the question felt strongly that he wanted a loyalty scheme and wasn't interested just in extra service. Sinclair turned the question to the audience, the majority of whom admitted to being customers of Pret à Manger. It came as some surprise perhaps to everyone present when a very large majority said they *didn't* want a loyalty scheme. They wanted something far more personal and less mechanical.

Sinclair's comments are equally relevant to customer referral incentive schemes as to loyalty programmes. Although Pret à Manger are looking to sell more to the same customers rather than get recommendations or referrals, he is clear in his mind that **exceptional service is far more powerful than incentive schemes**. Based on the audience reaction, it looks as though most of his customers agree with him.

That's not to say that incentive schemes don't have a role, but I would consider them to be a fairly passive approach, with the added downside that you are trying to inspire different personality types to refer you while you stick to one simple, general approach.

Although it is becoming less popular in many industries, financial incentives, introducers' fees (a reward to a contact for introducing a new customer) or commissions traditionally play a strong role in inspiring referrals. In fact, some commercial brokerages are purely set up as professional introducers, with their revenue coming solely or predominantly from introductory fees.

What is interesting is that a number of companies I have worked with have taken the decision to ban introducer fees, despite them being common currency in their industry. Such a move forces them to be more creative in inspiring people to refer them despite being unable to compete on price. To be successful in these circumstances, they need to focus on tailoring their approach to inspiring each individual champion, rather than just taking the one route to asking for referrals.

Another version of the introducer programme is *affiliate schemes*, which remain popular particularly where products are being referred.

Daniel Priestley has over 1,300 affiliates who promote his events business Triumphant Events. 'An affiliate programme allows you to track the source of a sale and then pay a commission to the originator of that sale,' said Dan. 'Effectively you only pay for marketing that gets you a result.

'Affiliate programmes are a dream come true for marketers. Rather than paying for distribution, you pay an allowable cost per sale, after the sale is made. This frees up your affiliates to market you in the way that's most effective – they blog about you, tweet about you, send emails to their contacts, update their groups and use social media – if done correctly your affiliate system allows people to communicate in the most effective ways to get you sales.

'To have a great affiliate system you need to make it reliable (people need to trust that they will get paid on time), transparent (they can see their results real time), engaging (they can log in and find tools and resources that make their job easier) and rewarding (they get a good commission/bonus if they do the work).'

some of your potential champions may be very transactional in personality

I certainly wouldn't advise against using transactional approaches to inspiring referrals. They have historically been very successful and have their place. In fact, some of your potential champions may be very transactional in personality and will only be inspired by the promise of reward.

Earlier this year I joined a small networking group of people in a similar industry. We agreed to meet regularly to support each other and, where possible, promote each other.

The question was asked whether we should have a formal agreement as a group to pay a commission on any referrals passed. Personally, I was happy simply to pass any referrals without thought of reward. If someone wanted a commission from an introduction to me, that would be fine.

Others in the group felt the opposite – that if they referred some business they should be rewarded for doing so. The thought of earning passive income was attractive.

Neither approach is right or wrong. It depends on what works for each individual and what the contact and the champion agree between them. In the end, we agreed not to have a formal rule for our group but to leave it to parties to agree their approach with each other on an individual basis.

If you do use more transactional approaches it certainly allows you to develop a more business-like approach to asking for referrals and chasing up connections you have been promised. As long as you ensure you offer a fair reward for business won, it can provide a win for both parties, and if someone is motivated by transactional rewards it's very straightforward to reinspire them to refer again.

If you run affiliate programmes to reward your introducers, you can set up uncomplicated systems to automate the tracking of referrals received and payment of commissions, just as Triumphant Events have demonstrated.

IN A NUTSHELL

Handled badly, transactional approaches to inspire referrals can risk relationships.

A word of warning, though: handled badly, transactional approaches to inspire referrals can risk relationships. Ensure you are transparent in all your dealings, both with your introducer and with your client.

Be very clear to introducers about what incentive is on offer and when it will be paid. If you will only pay commission when payment is cleared and it may be staggered, let them know that up front.

The right gift

Despite their nature, transactional inspirations can still be made personal. It is worrying how much wine and whisky is given out to teetotallers, or even just to people who prefer a different drink! Find out what motivates each individual and tailor your reward to their tastes, not your convenience.

find out what motivates each individual and tailor your reward to their tastes, not your convenience

Most importantly, only use transactional inspirations where appropriate. I was offered a financial inspiration to refer a close contact a couple of years ago. I refused the offer several times but still referred him because I was happy to do so.

Eventually, after much badgering to accept a 'thank you' cheque for what he told me was a very valuable referral, against my better judgement I relented. After all, I figured, the referral had already been passed and I might be turning down a substantial payment.

When I received a cheque for a nominal amount I simply felt insulted. For the same price he could have thanked me by sending across a nice bottle of Jack Daniels, showing that he knows what my favourite drink is, or taking me to a sports event. In fact, for a smaller amount he could have simply sent me a card saying 'thank you' and it would have made a more positive impact.

Instead of inspiring me to refer more, I have had little contact with him since and would be unlikely to refer him again. He has a transactional approach, mine is more relational. His failure to recognise the difference, despite several clear signals from me, has affected the likelihood of receiving referrals from me again. Above all else, I was happy to refer him without financial reward. Paying me to do so had no commercial value as I was more easily inspired in other ways.

RELATIONAL INSPIRATIONS

There are times when a transactional approach to obtaining referrals is the best course of action. This may be because of circumstances or the people involved. However, I believe that if you have developed a strong trusted network, relational methods will be far more effective.

The key is the strong, trusted network. If you are surrounded by people who want to help you, payment is often the last thing on their mind. In fact, many people report an equal 'buzz' from giving referrals as from receiving them.

It follows, therefore, that the first thing you need to do if you want to inspire people to refer you without payment is focus on your relationship with them. This shouldn't come as a surprise based on what else we've discussed in this book.

> many people report an equal 'buzz' from giving referrals as from receiving them

---

IN A NUTSHELL

Find out about the other person's needs. Discover who they would benefit from meeting and the information or resources they need to find. Make introductions that will make a difference to them.

When speaking with people, take yourself and your own needs out of the equation initially. Find out about the other person's needs. Discover who they would benefit from meeting and the information or resources they need to find. Make introductions that will make a difference to them.

THE 51-51 EQUATION

A few years ago I met with a business associate and friend, Servane Mouazan. Servane has a theory about networking which she calls 'the 51-51 equation'. Servane describes this as a way to measure and value your connections and your networking standards. Relationships which follow Servane's equation should result in benefits for both parties.

The principle is nothing new, but the equation is a very nice way of expressing the importance of the old adage of going the extra mile. If both parties in an interaction take one more step than that expected of them, the results will be a much stronger relationship and greater levels of trust and rapport.

Servane says that there are easy steps you can take to go beyond a 'flat 50%-50%'. As she puts it, 'This is the moment when secrets are revealed!'

The 51-51 equation is about going beyond what is expected and into the realms where you stand out from others and connect on a much deeper level.

If there are people in your network who have the opportunity to refer you and you want to develop their trust and willingness to refer, take the time out to meet them. Members of networking groups are regularly encouraged to meet outside events in one-to-ones.

When your goal in that one-to-one is to build the relationship, leave agendas to one side and get to know the other person. Find out what makes them tick and what matters, rather than concerning yourself with their business and only their business.

In his book *How to Win Friends and Influence People*, Dale Carnegie encouraged readers to 'become genuinely interested in other people'.[17] If you can find out about people's passions and show a genuine

> leave agendas to one side and get to know the other person

[17] Dale Carnegie (2009), *How to Win Friends and Influence People*. Simon and Schuster.

interest, you'll find yourself moving towards a stronger relationship much more quickly.

I was a participant on a training course once where we were split into groups for a series of role play exercises. The exercises were designed to make us recognise some of the situations where visitors to their events may feel uncomfortable and ill at ease. I was asked to play the role of visitor and approach one of the groups. What I didn't know was that the group had been asked to ignore me and repel me, physically if necessary.

I approached the group and was immediately met by a sea of backs and elbows (please don't try to work out how that can be physically possible and take my word for it!). Undeterred, I tried to start a conversation but was met with blank faces.

I knew that one of the members of the group, who was closest to me, had a keen interest in horses, as she had talked about it earlier in the day. My girlfriend at the time was a big horse enthusiast. I turned to the member and began to talk.

'By the way, I meant to chat to you about your horses. My girlfriend has a horse and loves riding,' I began.

Immediately her guard dropped, her face softened and her eyes came alive. For a split second, she forgot the exercise and her role in it and was ready to engage in conversation with me. She then remembered what she was supposed to be doing and started laughing.

When you meet someone new, you will inevitably have your guard up to some degree until you get to know each other. By engaging with someone's hobby, interest or passion you will see that guard drop very quickly and you can start the serious business of relationship building. If the woman I spoke to was in a position to refer me she would have been far more inclined to do so after I had shown an interest in her passion and wanted to engage in conversation about it.

> **IN A NUTSHELL**
>
> When you meet someone new, you will inevitably have your guard up to some degree until you get to know each other. By engaging with someone's hobby, interest or passion you will see that guard drop very quickly and you can start the serious business of relationship building.

There are simple steps you can take to demonstrate your interest in other people and stay in touch:

→ If you know what they are trying to achieve, invite them to relevant networking events you're attending.

→ Send regular emails, particularly if you spot something relevant to their interest.

→ Look for their status updates on social networks.

→ You could even be radical and resort to old technology, picking up the phone if you haven't spoken for a while!

AN EVENING OUT

Many people use corporate entertainment to keep in touch with their champions. In the UK you need to be aware, however, of the new Bribery Act 2010, which criminalises corporate hospitality 'where it was proved that the person offering the hospitality intended the recipient to be influenced or act improperly'.[18]

As long as you ensure that you act within the confines of the law, such entertainment will throw up a range of opportunities to invite people who could

[18] **http://www.iod.com/Home/Business-Information-and-Advice/ Being-a-Director/Hot-topics/Bribery-Act-2010---What-It-Means-For-Employers/**

refer you to functions such as charity dinners, sporting events and so on.

Sadly, many companies waste this valuable resource. It is important to understand how to use entertainment to inspire referrals. You need to invite the right people, focusing on who might be willing to refer you, and make sure you invite them to something they will be interested in rather than inviting them to events that you want to attend yourself.

For such entertainment to be effective as a way to inspire people to refer you, make sure you are clear that you don't automatically expect something in return. Remember, you are treating them and developing a relationship. Putting a price, or quid pro quo, on the gift conversely devalues the gesture.

For that reason, I wouldn't even raise the question of referrals while at the event.

In a networking forum last year, Aron Stevenson of UK-based Leasing Options asked for advice about how to engage with a high profile client they were inviting to attend a sporting event as their guests. Aron wasn't sure when would be the appropriate time to discuss business, if there was one at all.

My advice, along with that of others, was to focus on letting their guests enjoy the event without approaching the subject of business in general, or referrals in particular, there and then.

'I took the advice and made sure the day ran smoothly,' Aron later told me. 'We talked about sport, raising children and life in general. It was good to be able to relax and enjoy the game without expectation.

'My client had a great time and was very grateful for the invite. Since that game we have written additional business and I've been introduced to friends and work colleagues. My takeaway from this experience is that referrals flow naturally once you have developed trust and proved that you can deliver quality service.

> it is important to understand how to use entertainment to inspire referrals

'What I've learned from that experience is that trust must be built and developed first before moving on to referrals and working on other projects.'

MAKING IT WORTH THEIR WHILE

Normally taken to imply financial remuneration, you can make it worthwhile for people to refer you in other ways. Make sure that every time someone refers you it is a positive experience for them. It's quite simple really – if they feel positive about the outcome of a referral they have passed, they'll be more motivated to replicate the feeling.

> **IN A NUTSHELL**
>
> Make sure that every time someone refers you it is a positive experience for them. It's quite simple really – if they feel positive about the outcome of a referral they have passed, they'll be more motivated to replicate the feeling.

Treat the referrals you receive with the utmost importance. Follow up quickly and professionally; if you win the work, treat the customer as your most important and prized client. If you can't help, recommend or refer someone else if possible (check if your champion is happy for you to do so) and ensure you feed back why you weren't in a position to see it through.

If you lose the work, accept it gracefully and thank both the champion and the prospective client for the opportunity. The simple act of feeding back why the lead did not bear fruit will help your champion understand what may, or may not, be an appropriate referral for you, thereby increasing their understanding.

You may also get some valuable feedback from the prospect via the person who referred you, which the prospect would not share directly with you.

THE OBVIOUS . . . THAT SO MANY PEOPLE MISS

We'll finish with two of the easiest ways to inspire people to refer you, yet approaches that are often overlooked.

The first is referring them first. Don't wait for others to refer you. Find out what kind of introductions they need and, if possible, connect them. It's important not to expect referrals in return. As the early twentieth-century writer and poet Elizabeth Bibesco said, 'blessed are those who can give without remembering, and take without forgetting'.

don't wait for others to refer you

In many cases, you won't need to expect referrals in return. When receiving a gift (which a good referral is), people will generally feel obligated to respond without you demanding the response. In Chapter 11 we talked about Ivan Misner's theory of Givers Gain, and this is based on the same belief that most people want to return a favour.

The other obvious approach is to ask for the referrals you want. Unfortunately, many people do all the right things in building a strong network, but forget to ask for support.

A good friend of mine is a case in point. He has a tremendous reputation for his generosity. He is always looking to help others and goes out of his way to be amenable. This is despite the fact that his own business is struggling and he really needs to focus on his needs first. He said to me recently that if he doesn't win more business soon he may have to find employment and shelve his company.

It is possible that his amenability is actually a cause of his own struggle. My friend is so focused on seeking opportunities to help other people he forgets to ask for help for himself, or doesn't recognise opportunities for himself when they come along.

Last year I told him that I was going to introduce someone who could be very helpful in opening some important doors for his business. As soon as I described some of the projects this contact was working on, my friend began to list who he knew who could help on those projects.

> 'That's tremendous,' I said. 'But this is a connection for *you* and *your business*. You need to focus on that initially, don't lose the opportunity.'

> 'I know you're right,' he said. 'But I'm not greedy.'

> 'You've spent the last 12 years not being greedy. Maybe that's one reason you're so needy.'

His enthusiasm for helping other people in his network has got in the way of accepting much needed help for his own business.

He has a bank of people who he has helped and who would love to help him, but he doesn't feel comfortable asking for their help. As a result, they cannot recognise the right opportunities for him and he is struggling.

Givers Gain works on the understanding that your network will want to help you if you continue to help them. That only works, however, if they understand how to help you and if you accept that help when it comes your way.

It's fine not to be greedy, but not to the extent that it leaves you in need yourself.

RETAINING FOCUS

A referrals strategy requires a degree of focus. While you can make an effort to build stronger relationships with everyone around you and communicate your needs more clearly to them, it makes sense to spend some time developing specific referral relationships with a small group of people.

In theory, as long as a relationship is growing and remains positive, you shouldn't write off anyone as a referral source. However, if a lot of time and effort is required to develop the trust and understanding to a sufficient level for them to refer you, it is time perhaps to consider the return on that investment.

A harsh way to talk about relationships, perhaps, but necessary. If you are investing your business time and resources in cultivating relationships with the intention of generating referrals, you need to have a clear vision of what success will look like.

a referrals strategy requires a degree of focus

IN A NUTSHELL

If you are investing your business time and resources in cultivating relationships with the intention of generating referrals, you need to have a clear vision of what success will look like.

This is where the opportunity to refer we discussed in Chapter 6 is so important. Think about who people know and the conversations they are likely to have. Once they have reached a sufficient level of trust and understanding to refer you comfortably, are they in a position to refer you on a regular basis to the people you want to meet?

If so, carry on investing the time and effort to get to that stage. If they have a limited network and don't have the type of connections you are looking for, perhaps you should look elsewhere.

Ideal referral sources are in a position to keep introducing you to potential customers and other potential champions for your business. Your referrals strategy will be far more efficient if you develop strong bonds with 10 key people who each refer you 5 or 6 times a year, than if you try to build relationships with 50 or 60 people who might refer you once.

REVIEW

This chapter has covered the following:

1 Ensuring the key points are in place for people to refer you.

2 The difference between a transactional and a relational approach to referral generation.

3 The benefits and disadvantages of incentives.

4 Suggestions for developing a strong business relationship with your potential champions.

5 The importance of giving as well as receiving.

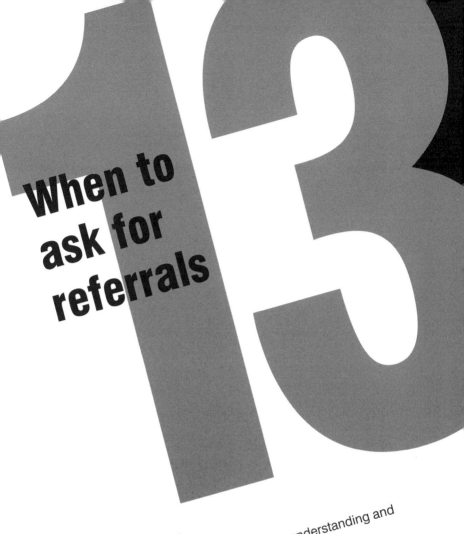

13

When to ask for referrals

→ When the time is *not* right

→ Ready to ask for that referral – timing, trust, understanding and opportunity to refer, all in place.

→ Making it as easy as possible for your champion to refer you

→ Using one-to-one meetings

WHEN *NOT* TO ASK FOR REFERRALS

Timing, of course, is everything. Goodwill and positive relationships can be destroyed by an ill-timed request for help. The value of everything you have put into a relationship can be diminished if it's seen to be done with an end in mind.

So, what are the warning signs?

The most obvious time to ask for referrals may appear to be when people ask you, 'How can I help?' In many cases this is an opportunity that you need to be able to respond to, but be sure that they are sincere first of all.

goodwill and positive relationships can be destroyed by an ill-timed request for help

In Chapter 6 I told you about an event where we were asked to offer our help to each other in a speed networking exercise, and the challenges associated with that. There are many people who, having been taught by people like me that they should show interest in others at networking events, will ask how they can help you immediately after shaking your hand for the first time.

You could, of course, take them up on their offer and ask for connections. But what help are you likely to receive? If they are not sincere, people are far less likely to follow up or give good quality connections. Without any understanding of your business or quality of service, the best you could hope for is a half-hearted introduction.

It may open a door for you slightly, but if they are genuinely willing to help someone they have just met, how much more powerful an introducer would they be once they have got to know you?

Don't forget, they will be offering their help on the understanding that the more they support others, the more likely it is that others will help them. While they may not demand something directly in return from you, the law of reciprocity does apply and you may well feel personally indebted to return the favour. Is it right to accept a referral if you wouldn't be willing to refer in return?

Two of the most common approaches to asking for referrals are either when people have just thanked you for a job well done, or at the end of a meeting with a client or prospect. The common wisdom is that if you have just done a good job or presented a good case, people will not only be happy to refer you but will be primed to do so.

In a twist on this approach, in his book *Influence: The Psychology of Persuasion,* Robert Cialdini refers to the 'rejection-then-retreat' technique used by door-to-door sales operations.

According to Cialdini:

> **the training programmes of each of the companies I investigated emphasised that a second important goal (for a door-to-door salesperson) was to obtain from prospects the names of referrals – friends, relatives or neighbours on whom we could call … in several such programmes I was trained to take advantage of the opportunity to secure referrals offered by a customer's purchase refusal …**

> **Many individuals who would not otherwise subject their friends to a high-pressure sales presentation do agree to supply referrals when the request is presented as a concession from a purchase request they have just refused.**[19]

I have described in detail earlier in this book why the information gathered in this way by the salespeople Cialdini trained with are not truly referrals. The target is typically to collect names and numbers of other people to approach and pitch for business – in other words, lead-generation, not referral-generation.

[19] Robert B. Cialdini (2007), *Influence: The Psychology of Persuasion.* Revised edition. Harper Business.

Even if you could collect referrals through any of these routes the timing is completely wrong. Whether someone has just thanked you for doing something to help them (either as part of your commercial relationship or just as a favour), or you have spent time demonstrating how your services can overcome their issues, you have been focused on them.

Having spent time focusing on your prospects, to then switch the focus back to you at the last minute destroys the impact you have made.

I make this point whenever I run a referrals workshop or discuss referrals strategy with a coaching client. I always ask them how comfortable they would feel if, after spending so much time focused on their business I suddenly turned around at the end and asked them for referrals. Not one person has told me that it would feel appropriate.

WHEN THE TIMING IS RIGHT

In my opinion, the best time to ask someone for a referral, assuming the basics covered earlier are all in place, is when you have something specific to ask for that is easy for your champion to fulfil.

> **IN A NUTSHELL**
>
> The best time to ask someone for a referral, assuming the basics covered earlier are all in place, is when you have something specific to ask for that is easy for your champion to fulfil.

The relationship you have built, the service you have provided and the support you have offered are all part of the process of building people's willingness to refer you. When trust and understanding are at the optimum level, take the opportunity to ask.

If you don't have a specific request to make, work out who your champion knows and how their network relates to the connections you need. If someone does ask how they can help and you know they mean it, be prepared, if necessary, to ask if you can come back to them, to give you time to think about the best request to make.

We've talked at length about the importance of making it easy for people to refer you. So focused requests are essential. Either people may have mentioned someone in their network who fits your ideal referral criteria or you have a specific target and have identified that they can help.

Once you know someone is ready to refer you and you know what you will ask them for, it's just a question of picking the right moment. In some cases you can simply pick up the phone and ask, particularly if it's just for one specific referral. With other people you may need to set a formal meeting to discuss referrals.

Many people who meet through formal business networks and find they have the seeds of a strong relationship arrange to meet for one-to-ones. The idea is to get to know each other better, find out more about each other's business and look to see if there are ways to help each other.

At some point in that relationship, and this will differ with everyone you meet, you will feel comfortable offering each other referrals, whether qualified or not. If you are in such a position, a one-to-one can be a very powerful environment in which to ask for help. You are both very focused on how you can help each other and are free to ask, and a number of referrals both ways can result. Just make sure that you don't offer to do anything you can't deliver, both in terms of time commitment and relationship.

> when trust and understanding are at the optimum level, take the opportunity to ask

With some champions you may also strike up a formal referral relationship. As a result of attending a course by the Referral Institute, I entered into one such relationship with a colleague. For the duration of the relationship we would meet once a month, get out our address books and run through details of people we knew. If either of us wanted an introduction to someone in the other person's network, all we had to do then was ask.

That particular referral relationship didn't last for long. It may have been because my partner's ideal referral was so niche and specific that I didn't need to sit down with him each month to know who to look for or that I just wasn't speaking to the right people. While it did last it did bring in some excellent business for me, though.

A fantastic way to ask for referrals is by using the social network LinkedIn. We will look at this in much more detail in Chapter 15.

REVIEW

This chapter has covered the following:

1 Recognising and responding to the opportunity to ask for a referral based on:
   - the right levels of trust
   - recognising when your champion is comfortable to refer you
   - knowing when the timing is right.
2 Understanding the power of the one-to-one.

Referring others with confidence

14

→ The importance of giving referrals, not just expecting to receive

→ Maximising opportunities at networking events

→ Listening and understanding

→ Effective timing and protecting your reputation

→ Recognising opportunities to refer

→ The analysis and power of a good introduction

→ Establishing the need and the right connections, then making the introduction

In the exercise in Chapter 12 I asked you to think about people you have referred in the past and to whom you referred them. When I run this exercise in workshops some people struggle to think of more than one or two people they have referred.

My question to them is always the same. How can you put a referrals strategy together where you expect other people to refer you, if you are not actively doing the same for them?

> **IN A NUTSHELL**
>
> How can you put a referrals strategy together where you expect other people to refer you, if you are not actively doing the same for them?

We have already talked about the concept of 'Givers Gain' in this book and no volume on referrals strategy would be complete without some advice on how to give referrals to other people. It is a two-way process and you will find that the more you seek to refer others, the more your reputation will grow as someone who connects people and the more likely it becomes that others will want to connect you too.

Much of what I will talk about in this chapter shouldn't come as a surprise. After all, it is merely a reflection of what we have already covered. If you understand how you want people to refer you, what motivates them and how to make it easy for them to do so, you are already a long way towards understanding how to refer others effectively.

SHOW A REAL INTEREST IN OTHERS

In Chapter 12 I talked about taking yourself out of the equation when you interact with people in your network. Rather than trying to sell to everyone you meet, or asking yourself how they are relevant to you as soon as you meet them, I've talked about the importance of establishing relationships and looking to help your contacts if possible and appropriate.

If you can reach the stage where you interact with people on a genuinely interested basis, you will find yourself making connections with ease. If you ask someone what they do, mean it. If that means not asking them until you are ready to know, don't automatically find out at the first time of meeting. I would usually try to get to know a person first.

if you ask someone what they do, mean it

When someone does tell you about their business make sure that you fully understand it. If they use jargon that means nothing to you, ask them to explain it in a different way. Do you really understand what they do, who they do it for, why people need their help? Could you confidently introduce them to someone else, explaining what they do in the process?

Ask them who they need to meet and, as you do so, think about other people in your network who might fit the bill. Get them to elaborate to help you understand how to recognise those people and why that person would want to meet them.

Find out how you can create a 'bridge' between the two parties. Remember our discussion on how to get your message across in Chapter 6? You are now the person having the conversation to set up the referral.

So, ask key questions that will help you feel comfortable with who you should refer them to and why that person would benefit from meeting them. Make sure you feel confident about the impending conversation before you try to pass the referral.

REFERRING OTHERS WITH CONFIDENCE

TACIT KNOWLEDGE

A key part of understanding about others is showing genuine curiosity and asking intelligent questions. If you ask about the challenges people face in their business, you might be able to identify other people in your network who are in a position to help them, or provide pertinent advice based on your own experiences.

> **IN A NUTSHELL**
>
> If you ask about the challenges people face in their business, you might be able to identify other people in your network who are in a position to help them.

Networking, after all, is about sharing and supporting. If people are comfortable sharing their problems and expressing vulnerability around you, the relationship and their trust in you will deepen. Just take care not to push them too far out of their comfort zone too soon.

networking is about sharing and supporting

John Hagel III, John Seely Brown and Lang Davison wrote about the importance of networking to share 'tacit knowledge' in the *Harvard Business Review* in January 2010.[20] 'In this world, it is not who you know, but what you learn from, and with, who you know,' they write.

According to Hagel, Brown and Davison, whereas classical networking approaches are focused on numbers of contacts, the power of your network to exchange experience and knowledge is much more reliant on long-term, trust-based relationships – exactly the type of relationships that we have been talking about in this book.

[20] This reference to the *Harvard Business Review* can be found at **http:// blogs.hbr.org/bigshift/2010/01/networking-reconsidered.html**

The authors go on to say:

> *In the classical networking approach, the game is about presenting yourself in the most favourable light possible while flattering the other person into giving you their contact information. This approach quickly degenerates into a manipulative exchange where the real identities of both parties rapidly recede into the background, replaced by carefully staged presentations of an artificial self. These staged interactions rarely build trust. In fact, they usually have the opposite effect, putting both parties on guard and reinforcing wariness and very selective disclosure.*

> *A learning disposition leads to a very different approach. Now the effort focuses on understanding the needs of the other, with a particular focus on understanding the biggest issues others are wrestling with. This requires intense curiosity, deep listening and empathy that seeks to understand the context that other person is operating in. It also requires willingness to disclose vulnerabilities, since it is often hard to get the other person to share their most challenging issues without a sense that you are willing to do the same.*

Developing such an approach means a number of things. You will find yourself establishing a greater empathy with other people in your network. The levels of trust between you will grow and, essentially for the purpose of this chapter, you will find yourself recognising many more opportunities to connect them to the people who can help overcome their challenges or grow their business.

THE ART OF LISTENING

The Swedish have a wonderful word. It is *lyhördhet* and it translates as 'listening with all of the senses'. In *and Death Came Third!* I talked about how we use the phrase 'listen to' in English, which for me suggests a passive act, and that we should instead 'listen for' people.

In *The Seven Habits of Highly Effective People*, Stephen Covey talks about 'empathetic listening':

> **'Seek first to understand' involves a very deep shift in paradigm. We typically seek first to be understood. Most people do not listen with the intent to understand; they listen with the intent to reply. They're either speaking or preparing to speak.**[21]

If you want to be a truly great networker and connector, you need to learn to 'listen for' people. This goes back to taking yourself out of the equation. Seek to understand how people in your network can help each other. Look for key words that connect them together, either based on their wants or needs.

IN A NUTSHELL

If you want to be a truly great networker and connector, you need to learn to 'listen for' people.

Take a step back and look at how you pigeonhole the people in your network at the moment. We discussed this in Chapter 9 when we looked at who's in your network and how you associate based on your relationship with them.

If you are truly going to take yourself out of the equation, you need to remove those pigeonholes.

[21] Stephen Covey (2004), *The Seven Habits of Highly Effective People*. Revised edition. Free Press.

Table 14.1 How can you help the people in your network?

NAME OF CONTACT	WHAT DO THEY DO?	WHO DO THEY NEED TO MEET?	WHAT ARE THEIR BIGGEST CHALLENGES?

Revisit the exercises we looked at in Chapters 6 and 9 and list the different people in your network. What do they do? What are their challenges? Who do they need to meet? (see Table 14.1.)

Look at the relationships between different groups and seek out associations. All of a sudden you may find that your cousin and the person you play golf with would both benefit greatly from being connected, yet it has never occurred to you because you relate to them in different ways; it's not relevant to the relationship you have with them.

WHEN TO REFER

Passing referrals to other people shouldn't be a time-consuming effort. You have your own work to worry about after all. Once you begin to understand how your network fits together and where opportunities for other people lie, it should soon become a natural part of your everyday activity to recognise those opportunities and connect people together.

There are two key factors to look at when deciding whether or not it is appropriate to pass a referral. The first factor is based on your reputation, the other your time and effort.

Safeguard your reputation

there are dangers in referring people too early in a relationship

There are, of course, dangers in referring people too early in a relationship. If people see you giving out referrals immediately, that help will be devalued. That is why I don't advocate asking people 'How can I help you?' when first meeting them at a networking event, or necessarily offering them a referral there and then.

You can, of course, pass 'qualified referrals', where you make it clear to the prospective customer that you have only just met the person. Even in these cases, a poor referral can affect your reputation and people may question your credibility if you pass these too often.

Make an effort to get to understand a person's needs and business first. Understand with whom they will find rapport and, particularly, whether they will act appropriately once you have introduced them.

Through a mutual acquaintance I connected with a well-known entrepreneur for the first time on an online social network. In our conversation, this entrepreneur mentioned that he wanted to meet 'interesting people'. I'm fortunate that I know a lot of interesting people, a perk of my job I suppose, and there are many people in my network I could see benefiting from an introduction to this individual.

However, I didn't make introductions straight away. Instead I arranged to meet with the entrepreneur and get to know him better. I wanted to know more about who he really needed to meet and who in my network he would get on well with. By doing so, I also feel I built my own credibility in his eyes, which in turn benefited the people I did introduce him to.

Once you have got to know people and their needs, and you are happy with the people you refer, your reputation will grow as you pass high quality introductions.

your reputation will grow as you pass high quality introductions

Look after your time and effort

The second factor is your own time and effort. I have quite a simple approach as to whether it is worth passing a referral, as illustrated in Figure 14.1.

If the effort you put in is low but the value to the person you are referring is likely to be high, for example, you just need to make a phone call and send an email to connect them to someone who needs their help, then simply pass the referral.

If the effort required from you is high and the likely value to your contact is low, it's probably best left alone.

In any other case, you need to decide on individual merit. If the value to them may be high but you need to do a lot of groundwork first, you need to weigh up

Figure 14.1 Knowing when to pass a referral

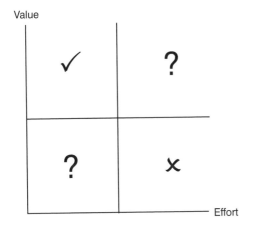

the pros and cons of doing so. If there is not much effort required but little potential value, it may not be worth following through, but it could be worth mentioning in case you're missing some of the likely benefit of the referral.

Remember, you may not always be in a position to know, or assume, the value of a potential referral so it is always better to pick up the phone and ask first.

WHAT WILL THE CONVERSATION LOOK LIKE?

Once you know who you are going to introduce, how are you going to do so effectively?

always explain the reason for the introduction

Sometimes it's as straightforward as asking someone if you can introduce them to a contact of yours who you think will be of benefit to them. Always explain the reason for the introduction, the problems you think your connection will resolve and the benefits of doing so. If you have a strong trust relationship then the other person should be receptive.

Unfortunately, it's not always that easy though. In other cases you need to establish the need before making the suggestion. Listen for 'trigger comments' that will suggest the problems your contact may resolve. You might be talking about the situation they are in or issues in their business.

IN A NUTSHELL

Listen for 'trigger comments' that will suggest the problems your contact may resolve.

If you are looking for opportunities to refer business to a recruitment consultancy, for example, you may recognise that such an introduction would be appropriate if someone mentions that they are planning to move office to accommodate more staff. Or they may mention that one or more of their key staff is leaving.

This comes back to the concept of 'listening for'. When people tell you about challenges in their business, or simply outline something that's happening, show a genuine curiosity. Ask them questions to establish the nature of the problem, how they are addressing it and then, if appropriate, make suggestions about how they might resolve it.

Obviously, the stronger the relationship you have the more probing you can be with your questions. Don't step over the line of comfort by interrogating someone you have only just met!

While you may not be selling the services of the person you are referring, it does help to have a reasonable understanding of their business and the service they provide. As already stated, in many cases you will find yourself overcoming initial objections and it helps to be able to anticipate questions that may arise.

Don't try to overcomplicate things, though. Where you are asked for more in-depth detail, that is the point to suggest making the connection. The aim is to get the person interested in hearing more.

MAKING THE RIGHT CONNECTION

Back in Chapter 1 I talked about one of the most common approaches to asking for referrals – where salespeople ask for the names and numbers of other people 'who may be interested' in what they do. I explained then how this was, at best, lead-generation.

In a similar vein, passing referrals is more than simply passing on a list of numbers and email addresses to people. And it is not enough to fire off an email to both parties unless you are absolutely confident that both will respond appropriately.

REFERRING OTHERS WITH CONFIDENCE

In Chapter 4 we established what a referral is. The key to a good quality referral is that the prospect is expecting a call from the person to whom you are referring them. The aim of your conversation is to get to that point. If you are comfortable enough to take it further, to the point where they are ready to buy, that's a wonderful bonus, but it's not the primary goal.

> **IN A NUTSHELL**
>
> The key to a good quality referral is that the prospect is expecting a call from the person to whom you are referring them.

be careful that you aren't trying to connect them with someone whose needs are too small

One of the most important things you can do is ensure you pass good quality information to both parties. It is important that they both know why they are being introduced and have both confirmed that the connection is potentially valuable.

That includes the recipient of the referral. Are you confident that the person you are referring them to *is* the type of client or introducer they are looking to work with and who will add value to their business? Be careful that you aren't trying to connect them with someone whose needs are too small, or too big, for them to profitably resolve. If necessary, pick up the phone to them first and check.

MAKING THE INTRODUCTION

Once you have established that both parties are interested in the connection, you merely have to put people in touch with each other. My preferred approach to doing so is an email to both parties, once I know they are both ready to talk. I keep it short and simple. After all, if I have done my job well all I need to say is:

> *Dear X and Y,*
>
> *Following our respective conversations, I am introducing the two of you as promised. You are both copied in on this email to introduce you and your contact details are:*
>
> *X – 0123 456789*
> *Y – 9876 543210*
>
> *Please do let me know how you get on.*
>
> *Kind regards …*

If necessary, I will add some extra information about the introduction, but I won't have to if I have spoken with both parties. If you are going to include telephone numbers, it's best to ensure you have permission to do so and use the appropriate number. Do they prefer to be contacted on their mobile phone, for example?

The benefit of this approach is that it gives the vendor the permission to follow up and contact their prospect. They know at this stage that their call is expected.

Another approach that you may wish to consider is to set up a meeting for the three parties involved, and that includes you. I know a number of people who favour this approach and it may be useful if one or both of the people you are introducing are key clients or contacts.

There can be a benefit for all concerned in you being there, but I would advise caution before going ahead with this approach as standard. It can be time consuming for you and makes it harder to organise the meeting when three diaries need to be synchronised. If you have strong relationships with and trust in both parties, how important is it to be there?

If you are due to meet with one of the parties separately, one solution is to invite the other party to join you towards the end of your meeting. You can then make the introduction and get out of their way.

Once you have introduced the two parties, keep in touch and find out how they have got on. That feedback can be so important for you to establish the value of each connection, the value you bring to your network and the reliability of the people you are referring.

REVIEW

This chapter has covered the following:

1 Developing the best use of networking events to establish relationships.

2 The difference between 'listening for' and 'listening to'.

3 Having the confidence to:
   − recognise opportunities to refer
   − know prospective clients for your contacts
   − choose the right time to refer
   − know how to motivate your contacts to make the referral.

4 Understanding the value of a good introduction.

5 Looking for trigger comments that will alert you to problems your contact might be able to resolve.

6 The importance of passing on good quality information to both parties.

7 Examples of making the introduction by:
   − email
   − meeting.

part 5

Tools you can use

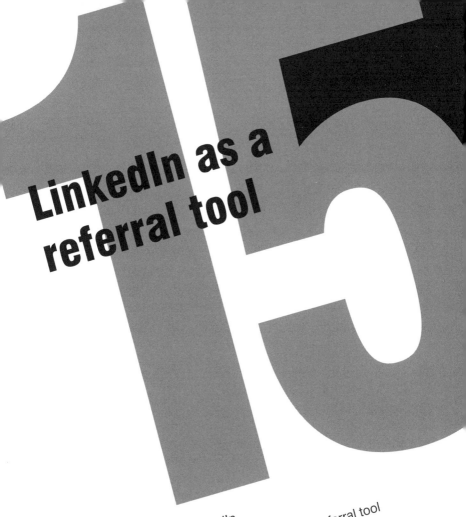

LinkedIn as a referral tool

15

→ How to make the most of LinkedIn

→ The four steps to using LinkedIn as an effective referral tool

Social networks have had a tremendous impact upon word of mouth marketing, both for good and bad.

From a positive perspective, there has never been such an inexpensive and accessible way to share your expertise and to help your network understand what you do and who you do it for. Whether through blogs, tweets, posts, forum comments or even video comment, the Internet has opened up a wealth of opportunity to get your message across.

IN A NUTSHELL

There has never been such an inexpensive and accessible way to share your expertise. Whether through blogs, tweets, posts, forum comments or even video comment, the Internet has opened up a wealth of opportunity to get your message across.

---

be proactive about which networks you use, and how you engage with them

It is one thing to be aware of social networks and their potential. If you are to implement an effective referrals strategy, however, you need to be proactive about which networks you use, and how you engage with them.

The network I want to focus on here is LinkedIn, as this is, in my opinion, the single most important online network for generating referrals.

Based on the six degrees of separation theory, LinkedIn helps users to see how they can connect with other members through mutual networks. Put simply, if you want to be introduced to someone else who is a member of LinkedIn, the site shows you the people you know who are connected to that person.

Six degrees of separation suggests that we are no more than five steps from anyone in the world. LinkedIn works on the first three degrees. You can see your network through the site. You can also get linked to your network's connections and even to another level beyond that. This is a very powerful tool if used properly and can allow you to ask for, and receive, important introductions.

FOUR STEPS TO USING LINKEDIN AS A REFERRAL TOOL

In this chapter I want to share with you the four straightforward steps to take to use LinkedIn as a referral tool. While there is plenty of other functionality on LinkedIn, and many ways to get value from the site, these four steps are all you need to know to get started and to get referred.

Not only are these steps easy to follow, once the initial work is done they should not take much time. If you have concerns about the time you have to spend online with sites like LinkedIn, think again. You could spend 10 minutes a day, or even 10 minutes a week, on the site and get powerful referrals for your business. How much time could that small investment save you elsewhere?

IN A NUTSHELL

If you have concerns about the time you have to spend online with sites like LinkedIn, think again. You could spend 10 minutes a day, or even 10 minutes a week, on the site and get powerful referrals for your business.

The steps outlined below are all available under the free membership category on LinkedIn.* There is additional functionality available for paying members, but that doesn't affect the advice I'm going to share with you here.

* Correct at time of publication.

STEP ONE – COMPLETE YOUR PROFILE

If you receive a referral from a connection on LinkedIn, where is the first place your new connection will visit to find out about you? If the referral takes place through LinkedIn, they will visit your profile first.

you must spend some time getting your profile right

That's why you must spend some time getting your profile right. It's not just a question of ticking the right boxes and putting in basic information. This is your opportunity to sell yourself. If a potential client is going to make a decision on whether or not they are interested in meeting you based on your profile, what do they need to see there?

> **IN A NUTSHELL**
>
> It's not just a question of ticking the right boxes and putting in basic information. This is your opportunity to sell yourself.

Here are a few things you may want to consider when writing your profile.

An engaging picture

LinkedIn is a social network; people want to engage with other people there. If you don't put a picture on your profile, you are falling at the first hurdle. That photograph needs to be professional but warm. Not a cold 'passport' head and shoulders shot, nor a more casual picture of you wearing a silly hat drinking a large beer! Some people use cartoons of themselves, but I don't think these are a suitable alternative either.

A clear message of what you do

When you edit your profile, underneath your name you will be invited to add a 'professional headline'. Unless your company name is well known or a brand you want to focus on, use this to share a statement that shows immediately the value you offer to others. Your company name won't mean much to others, nor will it invite immediate preconceptions, so use this field to capture the imagination of people reading your profile.

Your status

This should be updated regularly to keep your network informed about what you are doing (see Figure 15.1).

Figure 15.1   LinkedIn status update

Andy Lopata (you)
Turning networking and referral generation into serious business tools
Enfield, United Kingdom | Professional Training & Coaching

Andy Lopata Finalising work on my new book 'Recommended' before it goes to press
1 minute ago · Like · Comment · See all activity

'Professional experience and goals'

Use this field to write an engaging summary of your background and what you offer. I asked my LinkedIn network what they most liked about people's profile pages. The most common response was 'written in the first person'. Speak to people rather than at them in the summary and engage them in a way that they'll want to find out more. An example of this field is shown in Figure 15.2 (overleaf).

Figure 15.2 Professional experience and goals field on LinkedIn

Summary

KEYNOTE SPEECHES - CONSULTANCY - TRAINING

"One of Europe's Leading Business Networking Strategists" - The Financial Times

"Mr Network" - The Sun

I believe that networking is a vital tool in business, from sales generation to career development. Unfortunately, it's still not treated with the same strategic consideration as other business methods, leaving many companies and individuals failing to realise the potential their networks offer.

By knowing why you are networking and what you want to achieve, it is possible to plan accordingly and get great, measurable results.

A business networking strategist, I work with companies on how to use networking tools to develop their businesses. Networking is not just about sales. Whether for lead generation, breaking down silos internally, recruitment and retention of top staff or developing future leaders, networks and collaboration have a key role to play. I work with my clients to help recognise that role and put the strategy and skills in place to leverage it.

I have a regular column for the US magazine 'The National Networker' and have been quoted in national press, including The Sunday Times, The Financial Times and The Guardian. I have also co-authored two books on networking, with a third being published in Summer 2011.

For eight years, I was Managing Director of Business Referral Exchange, one of the UK's leading referral-focused networking groups with over 2,000 member companies. I now work with companies from one-man bands to global names such as the BBC, Sage and Mastercard to help them realise the full potential from their networking.

Specialties

Business networking strategy. Referral strategy, Social networks

'Specialities'

Search engine experts will tell you to use key words here to help you get found, as well as elsewhere on your profile. That is fine but not my focus here. However else you use your profile, you should make it clear in this field how you can help people and when they should be thinking of you.

Current and past positions

Make sure all relevant current and past positions are included, with a brief description of what was involved. Ask yourself again what people need to read here to make them want to meet with you.

STEP TWO – BUILD YOUR NETWORK

The first thing to note is that this is step two, not step one. If you are going to connect with people you may not have seen for a while, just like your prospects the first place they will look is your profile. So get that right first before moving on to this stage.

Building your network is an important part of using LinkedIn to generate referrals, but it's not simply a question of 'size matters' here. There is a group of 'LinkedIn Open Networkers', who build their networks as large as possible on the basis that this increases the number of connections they have, and they might disagree with me. But I believe you need to restrict your connections to people you know, like and trust if you are looking for referrals.

it's not simply a question of 'size matters'

> **IN A NUTSHELL**
>
> If you approached someone and asked them to introduce you to a trusted contact, would they be happy to do so? And if they asked you to refer them, how would you feel?

There's a rule of thumb for me. If you approached someone and asked them to introduce you to a trusted contact, would they be happy to do so? And if they asked you to refer them, how would you feel? If there is any unease, perhaps there is more relationship building to be done before you connect on LinkedIn.

However, for the site to work effectively for you to generate referrals, you need to build a critical mass. Restricting yourself to 10 connections of your nearest and dearest is not going to give you the reach you need for LinkedIn to meet its full potential. On the flip side, trying to work your way through 10,000 connections, with or without the help of the site's search engine, could make LinkedIn a much less efficient tool.

Use the tools on the site to upload the contacts from your email account. You then will have the opportunity to decide who on the uploaded list you'd like to invite to join you on LinkedIn.

My advice is to ensure that all the connections are deselected first (that means you do not have a tick beside them). Then go through the list and invite the people who satisfy the relationship criteria I've discussed above. I wouldn't advise sending invitations to people who aren't already members of LinkedIn without checking with them first. By this stage they are probably tired of all of the invitations they've received.

You will find that you start to get more and more connection requests from people you don't know on LinkedIn. The site suggests people to fellow members who they may know, based on mutual connection, previous correspondence and other factors. Many people simply click 'connect' in these cases. I strongly urge you not to do so without filtering.

if you feel there is value in connecting with someone then do so

If you feel there is value in connecting with someone then do so, but make sure you strike up a conversation with them too so that you can begin to develop a meaningful relationship.

If you do send messages to people to connect, add a personal note to each one. You can change the templates provided by the site. And if you receive invitations from people you don't know or don't want to connect to, don't just delete them.

IN A NUTSHELL

If you receive invitations from people you don't know or don't want to connect to, don't just delete them.

Instead, reply explaining why you don't want to connect and, if possible, inviting them to connect on another site, such as Plaxo. I always like to offer an opportunity to connect somewhere. They may genuinely be looking to build a relationship and look for opportunities in the long term. By simply 'ignoring' them you may lose a positive contact.

by simply 'ignoring' people you may lose a positive contact

You may, of course, want to expand your connections to new people who might be potential champions or who add value to your network in other ways.

Tim Bond, managing director of NetworkingSunday. com, who helps businesspeople manage their *LinkedIn* strategy, advises building connections with people through Groups, using the fact that you are both members of the same group to approach them.

'As long as there is mutual interest,' says Tim, 'in many cases professionals will be keen to talk, providing your profile page gives them the information and confidence they need to respond. If you share a *LinkedIn* Group with someone then you can send them a message and initiate conversation.

'Join *LinkedIn* Groups where prospective customers and partners are likely to be members (the maximum number of Groups you are allowed to join is 50, so make sure you join them all to maximise reach). Balance memberships between the large industry and the smaller specialist groups related to your business.'

If you do decide to build your network beyond your trusted circle, remember that you need to build those relationships if your new contacts are going to feel comfortable about referring you. Don't just make the connection request and smile softly to yourself when it's accepted. From that point you need to start the conversation and keep in touch. When you need to approach your new contact for their help, will they feel happy and comfortable to offer it?

STEP THREE – THE POWER OF ENDORSEMENT

It's one thing for you to say what you are good at; it's something else entirely when other people do it for you. LinkedIn, along with a number of other social networks, makes it easier than ever to collect endorsements from people who you have worked for, who have worked for you or who you have worked alongside.

Look at the people you have connected with and ask yourself which ones have the right story to tell. You are not looking for people who can say how nice or what good fun you are. You need testimonials that will encourage prospective clients to find out more and accept your connection request.

IN A NUTSHELL

Ideal testimonials should share the value you bring to the people you work with.

Ideal testimonials should share the value you bring to the people you work with (see Figure 15.3). Ideally the person giving the testimonial will have faced a challenge you have helped them overcome and can tell the story of how you did that and what benefit they enjoyed as a result.

Figure 15.3 Testimonial on LinkedIn

"Andy is one of my networking gurus - he's my go-to point for any questions or queries relating to networking, networking techniques and networking problems - whether it's face to face networking or online.

He's an engaging and pragmatic speaker and clearly shares his knowledge of networking with an audience and brings them into the conversation - tackling tricky networking issues in a no-nonsense way that is really useful in terms of developing your own networking expertise.

I wouldn't hesitate to recommend Andy as a speaker and indeed have done many times before and will continue to do so in the future!" *February 21, 2011*

(1st) Maggie Berry, *Managing Director, womenintechnology.co.uk*
    was with another company when working with Andy at Andy Lopata - Business Networking Strategy

I'd recommend you asking for a handful of strong testimonials telling the right story rather than masses of testimonials that fail to add any additional value. LinkedIn allows you to ask people to amend testimonials they have written for you before you post them on your profile – don't be afraid to ask them to do this.

You need the testimonials you do publish to have the right impact. Your prospective connections won't read each and every testimonial posted unless you only have a handful, so each one has to count.

Just because people give you a testimonial, don't feel obliged to give one in return. You may not have experienced their services in the same way, especially if they were clients of yours, and your testimonial may not add the same value to their profile. Additionally, many people are sceptical if they see two parties exchanging testimonials with each other. They begin to doubt their authenticity.

just because people give you a testimonial, don't feel obliged to give one in return

STEP FOUR – SEARCHING FOR CONNECTIONS

You now have a profile that will engage, people who will connect you and the third party endorsement to back up your claims. You are ready to look for referrals.

There are two main ways I look for referrals on LinkedIn.

Within your own network

The first is simply to look at the network of your connections. LinkedIn allows you to see the networks of the people you have connected to, as long as they haven't chosen to hide it (and why would you if you only connect to people you trust?).

One word of reassurance: you can't see the networks of people you are not directly connected to; therefore they in turn can't see yours.

You're unlikely to want to trawl through everyone in the network of each of your connections. The larger your network the more of a chore this could be. But if you have identified someone who would be happy to refer you, or someone has offered their help, you have the opportunity to see who they know and how they might best be able to help you.

Outside your own network

Better than inside your own network, I believe that the more efficient route is to search for connections outside your own network. Using LinkedIn's search fields you can look for people by name, company, job title or location. If you want to meet someone in marketing at Ford within 50 miles of London, then search using those terms. Figure 15.4 is an example of a LinkedIn search I made recently to achieve just that.

Figure 15.4   LinkedIn search tab

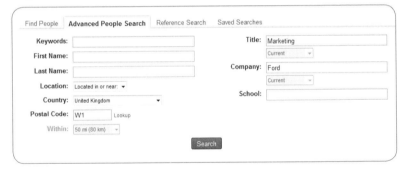

Running the exact search shown in Figure 15.4 gave me 35 results of people who satisfy the criteria. I can reach out to 23 of them through my existing connections. Within those 23 may well be the person I need to speak to if I want to work with Ford.

If you have a connection to them, alongside each name will be a blue circle. Inside the circle it will say 1st, 2nd, 3rd or Group. That means that you either are already connected to that person (1st), know someone who is (2nd), know someone who knows someone who is (3rd) or are in the same LinkedIn Group as them.

Figure 15.5 is an example of the result of my search in Figure 15.4. You can see that the person is a third degree connection.

Figure 15.5   Example of LinkedIn search results

Mark S. ⟨3rd⟩		Send InMail
Marketing Director at Ford Motor Company Limited		Get introduced
Chelmsford, United Kingdom | Automotive		Add to network
		Find references
		Save profile

If they are a second degree connection, you can click below their name to see who you know who can introduce you. If they are a third degree connection, click on 'Get Introduced' and it will tell you which of your connections can provide the next link in the chain.

ASKING FOR THE REFERRAL

Once you understand how you can connect with someone, it just remains for you to ask for the introduction. You can either do this by picking up the phone and asking your contact direct, or by asking through the site.

One of the biggest problems we encounter when we ask for referrals is that we are not in control of the conversation that takes place when the referral is actually made. All we can do is educate our champion well and hope that they are able to repeat the message clearly enough to spark some interest in our prospective client.

> **IN A NUTSHELL**
>
> On LinkedIn we can manage the initial approach to a prospect much more effectively, by writing it ourselves.

On LinkedIn we can manage the initial approach much more effectively, by writing it ourselves. When we ask for an introduction we are asked to write two messages. The first message is to the person we are asking to pass on the connection. If they are then passing it through someone else in their network, they will write their own personal message to them. The second message is to the person we want to be connected to. This can be seen by all the links in the chain, allowing them to decide whether they are happy to forward it. Figure 15.6 is an example of the LinkedIn screen you can use in order to kick-start the referral process.

consider what may make them *want* to respond

Think carefully about both messages before you write them, particularly the one to your prospective client. Consider what may make them *want* to respond. Will the person or people passing on the referral be comfortable passing it on?

I once received a request to connect someone in my network with a celebrity chef in the network of someone else I knew. The message they asked me to pass on was, 'If you ever need someone to look at your pension arrangements, give me a call'.

Suffice to say, I didn't pass on the connection.

Figure 15.6   Referral screen on LinkedIn

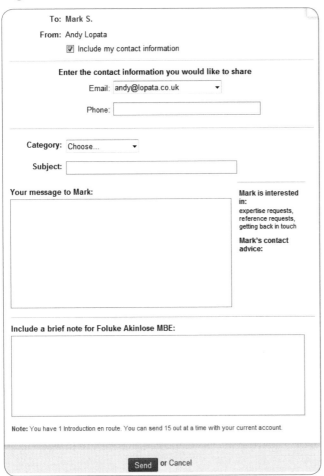

THE MAGIC EMAIL

Jan Vermeiren, the author of *How to REALLY use LinkedIn*, believes that you shouldn't use the onsite functionality to ask for a referral. Instead, Jan favours what he calls the 'Magic Email'.

'The first step,' says Jan, 'is to call the person you have in common and ask about the relationship he has with the person you are interested in. This is crucial since some people just accept any invitation and don't actually know other people personally. As a consequence their introduction won't be worth much. If the person you are calling is not the right one, then call your next common contact.

'Once you have found a good contact, ask them to write a Magic Email. Do this by asking them: "Can you connect me to person X by introducing us to each other in one email?"'

So, why is this email 'magical'? Jan notes that the two main reasons are:

→ 'Since the "middle man" took the time and the effort to write the email the recipient will be more open to talk to you. You are already "presold". Depending on the relationship between the two of them and between you and the "middle man" this can already be enough.

→ You don't have to write about yourself. Many people don't like to promote themselves or don't do it in a way that is compelling to the recipient. A third party introduction is much more powerful.'

HOWEVER YOU DO IT, JUST ASK

There are strong arguments for both approaches and I personally use a mix of requests through the site and simply picking up the phone to your mutual contact as favoured by Jan.

Either way, LinkedIn can provide the perfect tool for bringing together much of the guidance in this book and asking for referrals. Once you have done the groundwork and have a strong profile, network and testimonials, it's up to you just to ask.

Sadly, that's where most people fall down.

Do you have a list of companies or industries you'd like more work in? Then try it out now. Search for people in those areas on LinkedIn and, as long as you have a fairly strong network, you may be surprised at how connected you are.

you may be surprised at how connected you are

What difference would it make to your business if you spent just 10 minutes a week asking for such connections, from people who would be happy to pass them on?

REVIEW

This chapter has covered the following:

1 The steps you need to take to make using LinkedIn an effective method of referral-generation.

2 The four most important procedures:
   - completing your profile
   - building your network
   - understanding the power of endorsement
   - searching for connections.

3 How to use the 'Magic Email'.

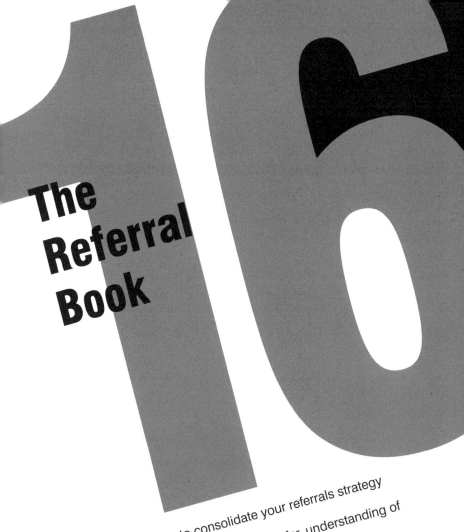

16

The Referral Book

→ Using the Referral Book to consolidate your referrals strategy

→ Your champions and their willingness to refer, understanding of your business and opportunity to refer

→ Specifying the introductions and support you are looking for – who do they know and how could they help?

→ Inspiring and motivating your champions

→ Tracking referrals

The Referral Book follows a simple process, based on the areas covered in this book, which allows you to identify potential champions, work out how to inspire them and what support you should be asking them for. It then helps you follow referrals as they come in through to their outcome and the feedback you offer.

Let's look at the Referral Book process step by step.

YOUR CHAMPIONS

To get you started, my advice is to start with the names of five people who you would like to see refer you on a regular basis. Think of people who have the opportunity to refer you, people who you know immediately want to refer you or people who have a good basic understanding of what you do.

If you need a refresher on any of these aspects, you can refer back to Part 2 of this book.

Your potential champions could be business contacts, friends, family members or people you've only met once but are perfectly placed to help. List them in Table 16.1.

Table 16.1 Referral Book – your champions

NAME OF CHAMPION	WILLINGNESS TO REFER (1–10)	UNDERSTANDING (1–10)	OPPORTUNITY TO REFER (1–10)

Now we need to look at each of your champions in turn. Before turning to them and asking them to refer, we need to understand how ready they are to do so. This knowledge will guide your next steps.

Picture yourself in a conversation with your potential champion. Now imagine yourself in their shoes. You have just asked them if they would be happy to refer you. How do they feel? Try to get a sense of their gut instinct. Are they keen to find out how they can help? Are they prepared to help but not overly enthusiastic? Or are they noticeably uncomfortable at the thought?

When you have a sense of how they feel, you need to score them for their *willingness to refer*. Give them a score out of 10, where 0 means they are not prepared to refer you at all (in fact, they'd be more than happy to tell people *not* to use your services) and 10 means they are desperate to help.

Now try to recognise how they would refer you and picture the conversation they would have with a good prospect for your business. Are they able to recognise that person as a prospect for you in the first place? If they do, what do they say to them and with what ease and confidence can they raise the subject and convince the other person that they would be interested in speaking with you?

Based on their ability to recognise and convert opportunities for you, you can give them a similar score out of 10 for their *understanding* of your business.

You also need to think about the conversations they are having. Who are they talking to and about what? Do they socialise or do business with the people you'd like to meet? If so, are they talking about the types of issue or problem that you can resolve, and would their judgement be trusted if they proposed speaking to you to provide a solution?

By understanding your champion's network and the conversations they are having, you can recognise

picture yourself in a conversation with your potential champion

their *opportunity to refer* you. If they are constantly talking to your prospective clients about problems you can solve, you'd score them a high 10. If they never meet your prospects, let alone speak with them, they'd score a zero and perhaps you should be focusing your activities elsewhere.

WINNING REFERRALS

Once you know how well placed your champions are to refer you, you can start to look at the specific help you want to ask them for and also how to get to a position where you are comfortable doing so.

We have talked at length about the importance of specific requests and how these make it so much easier for other people to refer us. Having identified your champions and their networks in the previous exercise, you should now be in a position to specify the introductions and support you'd like from them (see Table 16.2).

Table 16.2 Referral Book – winning referrals

WHO DO THEY KNOW?	HOW COULD THEY HELP?	METHOD OF INSPIRATION	REFERRALS REQUESTED/ PROMISED

I have included questions on both *Who do they know?* and *How could they help?* because the support your champion can initially offer may not be referrals but key market knowledge, feedback on your ideas or other suggestions. You need to be open to all possibilities before you get the ideal referrals at the right time.

> **IN A NUTSHELL**
>
> The support your champion can initially offer may not be referrals but key market knowledge, feedback on your ideas or other suggestions.

For each champion you could list two or three individuals or business types they might know. Don't make the list too long initially. Keep it focused. As they begin to refer you and show a willingness to continue to do so, you can always add more potential introductions to the list.

Now you need to ask yourself what your next step is to turn a contact into a champion. The scores you gave them for *willingness to refer* and *understanding* should give you a clue about the *method of inspiration* you next need to take.

ask yourself
what your
next step
is to turn a
contact into
a champion

If they are less than willing to refer, it is important that you focus your efforts on building their trust first. After all, if they don't want to refer you, why would they be interested in understanding more about your business? Work out what you'd need to do next to start developing more trust. Perhaps you need to invite them out for a coffee or a meal, find out more about their business or help them overcome their challenges.

Decide on which step seems appropriate and make the necessary arrangements. Once you have seen how effective that action has been, you can work out what your next step needs to be.

Once they are *willing to refer*, do they *understand* what you do well enough to *recognise opportunities*? If not, what do they need to know? To build *understanding* you may choose to introduce them to some of your clients so that they can find out more about how you helped them. It may be easier to share some case studies with them or invite them to see you working if appropriate.

Each *method of inspiration* will lead to another and then another until your champion is ready and able to refer. At that time all you may need to do is *ask* them for a referral.

once you ask people for referrals, it is important to keep track of those referrals

Once you ask people for referrals, or they promise to make a connection for you, it is important to keep track of those referrals. So often introductions are mentioned during a long conversation and then forgotten by one or both parties. By making a note of *referrals requested and promised* you are able to go back to your champions and ask how they are progressing, or gently remind them, if nothing comes through.

Please note that this isn't the same as nagging or harassing once the promise has been made!

TRACKING RESULTS

As your referrals strategy starts to pay dividends, you can track the *referrals received* (see Table 16.3). On an individual basis this drives you to *follow up* each referral received and makes sure you reach some kind of, hopefully positive, conclusion.

Your champions will regularly ask you what happened to the introductions they made for you. By tracking your follow-up, you can easily see what the last action was and also make sure you don't let anything drop. This is also a useful tool for sales managers and directors to see how well their teams respond to referrals received; something that otherwise can often

Table 16.3 Referral Book – tracking results

REFERRAL RECEIVED	FOLLOW UP	RESULT	FEEDBACK / THANK YOU

lead to conflict if the people generating the referrals and those tasked with following them up are different.

Noting the *result* of the referrals you receive achieves a number of things. First of all, you can tell how much business you get through your referral sources. You can also tell which referrals are more likely to turn into business and which sources are most effective for you.

In addition, you know when and how to *feed back* to your champion. I strongly believe that a lot of business is lost simply because we forget or neglect to give people who give us referrals effective feedback and fail to thank them for their support. This is probably the simplest area of any referrals strategy and yet the most easily overlooked.

> **IN A NUTSHELL**
>
> A lot of business is lost simply because we forget or neglect to give people who give us referrals effective feedback and fail to thank them for their support.

Even if a referral doesn't work out, you should be providing your champions with feedback. For starters, it makes them feel valued whatever the outcome. On top of that, you are helping them understand which referrals work for you and which don't and how they might make more effective referrals in the future.

THE REFERRAL BOOK AS A TOOL

A tool like the Referral Book allows you to capture some valuable information, but it should be used in a more creative way than that. If used properly it should tell you a series of stories, about the people you want to introduce you, how you turned them into your champions through a series of actions, the referrals you asked them for and how easy it was to turn those referrals into business.

anyone else in your business should be able to pick up your Referral Book

Anyone else in your business should be able to pick up your Referral Book and see how different introducers can help the business in different ways, and which inspirations tend to be most successful with different groups of people.

One of my clients has developed a different Referral Book for each channel of introducers so that they can focus on each in different ways and easily see which patterns emerge.

You should also be able to find out how many referrals you need to close business and how well you are getting your message across to your network.

> **IN A NUTSHELL**
>
> Constantly review and monitor the activity in your Referral Book and change your behaviour, or even your champions, accordingly.

It will only work like this, however, if you put aside the time to use it effectively. Constantly review and monitor the activity in your Referral Book and change your behaviour, or even your champions, accordingly. Work out whether you are getting a return on your activity, whether you are being complacent by doing the same things for the same champions time and again and where you need to adapt your approach.

Of course, as people start to refer you regularly, you can see that happen and the types of referral they are offering. Once those come automatically and you know that they understand that part of your business well enough, you can try to expand their knowledge and look for other types of referral as well. All of a sudden, someone who has already demonstrated that they are happy to refer you regularly is in a position to do so even more.

REVIEW

This chapter has covered the following:

1   Guidelines to produce a written record of your referrals strategy and those champions most likely to produce referral opportunities for you.

2   The importance of monitoring and updating your information to make the most effective use of it.

3   The Referral Book as a valuable tool in increasing your business opportunities.

17

Results you can rely on

→ Tracking results and refining the message

→ Taking the long-term view – a referrals strategy

→ Return on investment and forecasting results from your referrals strategy

→ Reigniting the flame

→ Conversion rates

TRACKING THE RESULTS

A strategic approach to your word of mouth marketing involves measuring what is already happening and tracking the results you achieve. By doing that a salesperson can recognise who their top sources are and what works best, while a sales director can identify who in their team is effectively generating new business through their network.

If you keep a record of each referral you receive from every source and track back new business to its originator, you can then focus your time and effort on proven referral sources, creating more efficient results. After all, once people have shown a willingness to refer and the understanding to do so, shouldn't you be doing all you can to encourage and enable them to do so more often?

By tracking your interactions with your champions, you can easily identify those approaches which are more effective than others. You can then both replicate them as appropriate with future champions and help other people, in both your organisation and your network, understand how they can also generate more referrals for their business.

looking at what has gone before, you can refine your message

To take it a step further, you will be able to break down the new business generated by type of introducer or type of prospect. Looking at what has gone before, you can refine your message. Try alternative methods of asking for referrals; describing your prospect and their needs in different ways.

Most importantly for many businesses, you can use the feedback from your referral tracking to demonstrate the return on investment that it is producing. Many networking events and meetings with key people in your network show little in the way of short-term results.

> **IN A NUTSHELL**
>
> A referrals strategy is focused more on the long
> term, with the aim being to produce year on year
> results from networking.

A referrals strategy is focused more on the long term,
with the aim being to produce year on year results from
networking. That isn't easy to sustain in a sales culture
where performance and activity are driven by immediate
goals and the need to generate revenue now.

You will need time to produce the evidence that can
justify time spent networking and building relationships.
Tracking your referral activity will ensure that you can
easily see where much of your time and effort is going
and whether the return is a fair reflection. But don't
forget that networking needs a long-term approach and
you must ensure you set fair goals for a realistic return.

Working with a sales team recently, I was asked by
one delegate why he should shift attention from his
traditional cold-calling activity to more networking and
referral-generation.

I responded in two ways. First of all, as already
stated earlier in this book, I believe that if cold-calling
produces a positive return on investment, referral
activity can complement rather than replace it.

I also advised him to look to a more gradual shift
in his activity. Instead of focusing 100 per cent of his
time on cold-calling, he should incorporate some
networking and referral activity into his agenda and
start to build a network of people who will support him.
Moving focus from one to the other too quickly would
simply lead to him trying to sell at networking events,
which would be counter-productive.

RESULTS YOU CAN RELY ON

So I suggested, in the short term, relying on cold-calling for sales and building a network separately. Over time he would be able to turn to his network for more and more referrals, at which time he would start to see the benefit of such a strategy. But patience is the key.

FORECASTING

Once you have a good tracking system in place and can see a strong indication of where your best referrals come from and in what situations, you can start predicting how much business can be expected from each source. That becomes invaluable when setting your business plan for the following year and also establishing what return on investment you expect from your networking and word of mouth marketing activities.

> **IN A NUTSHELL**
>
> Without a strategy that incorporates such tracking, referrals will tend to be far more random and less predictable, making it much tougher to come up with accurate forecasts for the business.

one of the biggest challenges is the failure of businesses to allocate sufficient resources to networking

Without a strategy that incorporates such tracking, referrals will tend to be far more random and less predictable, making it much tougher to come up with accurate forecasts for the business. With a clear picture of where your referrals will come from, you can begin to set increasingly higher goals and work out how to achieve them.

One of the biggest challenges facing people seeking to pursue a referral-generation strategy at present is the failure of businesses to allocate sufficient resources to networking.

When I was running networking groups we saw the ridiculous sight of bank managers, who had been generating good returns, resign their membership because the bank no longer had the ability to pay for their weekly breakfast. In fact, most bank managers I spoke to were finding the resources for membership from other budgets, at the cost of another key activity. Such scrimping is not conducive to generating strong results, or even to running a business effectively.

Being able to forecast the return on investment from such networking activity will help you to make the business case for the resources you need to run an effective referrals strategy.

BRINGING YOUR CHAMPIONS BACK INTO THE FOLD

With most current referral-generation being *reactive* – in that it happens to you rather than you make it happen – there is little chance to learn from what works and manage your behaviour so that you can improve the return from your connections.

Once you have strong measurement tools in place, however, this changes. As you build up a picture of where referrals have come from and how they came about, you can be *proactive* in making sure that you maximise the potential offered by your network.

The first thing you can look to do is identify lapsed champions and take the appropriate action to encourage them to start referring you again. After all, they have already shown the ability to refer you and the will to do so. In most cases you may find they have stopped simply because of your failure to maintain the relationship, and it can be easily reignited.

I ask many teams I run workshops for to call a lapsed referral source in the break. On many occasions we have found out that the source thought they had left their position because they hadn't heard from them and have given them new referrals instantly.

you probably haven't noticed who has stopped referring you

At present you probably haven't noticed who has stopped referring you – not unless you have stopped to think about it, which most people haven't. When you track the results of your referrals strategy, you can see when people have stopped referring you by looking at patterns of referral behaviour.

It's easy to identify when you might have become complacent. Perhaps you have assumed they would refer automatically anyway, have forgotten to keep in touch or simply have not changed your behaviour towards them in order to encourage and sustain those referrals. If you want to continue to motivate your champions you need to *do* something, often. Be proactive.

Once you can see where the problem lies, you can then change your behaviour to reignite the conversation and bring them back into the fold.

REPLICATING EXISTING SUCCESSES

Understanding the behaviour that leads to successful referral sources will also help you to develop further champions. A Referral Book, recording your relationship with the key people who refer you, will allow you over time to look out for patterns. Those patterns show you how to do two things, replicate those successes and, if you run a sales team, train others to do the same.

Initially your attempts to identify the right people to refer you and to inspire them to do so may be hit or miss. You will need to try different things with different people, finding out what works or learning from less positive experiences.

After a while, however, you can start to recognise patterns. It may be that certain approaches always seem to be successful with a particular type of introducer, or you identify a question that consistently yields results.

Another pattern to look out for is in the type of people who successfully refer you. Once you establish that people in a particular industry, or whom you meet through a particular network, for example, regularly offer you good quality referrals, you may decide to focus more of your efforts in that direction and replicate the success.

As you build up a picture of what successfully works with more than one champion, and which groups of people refer consistently, you can then create a system that allows you both to duplicate your actions with other potential champions and to pass it on to others to implement for themselves.

HOW MANY REFERRALS DO YOU NEED TO MAKE A SALE?

One other area that I have touched on earlier is the importance of understanding conversion rates. Don't make the mistake of thinking that each referral will lead to completed business. You are very lucky if that is the case. What referrals should give you is a greater chance of winning business from the introduction, but you will still have referrals that don't succeed.

Through your Referral Book you can start to build up a picture of how many referrals lead to meetings and from how many of those meetings you win business. It will be interesting to compare these results with the same data from other routes to market such as enquiries through your website and cold-calling.

don't make the mistake of thinking that each referral will lead to completed business

RESULTS YOU CAN RELY ON

make sure you ask for enough referrals to win the business you need

Once you know what your conversion rate is, there are two things you need to do. The first is to make sure you ask for enough referrals to win the business you need, based on the conversion rate you've identified.

The second is to improve the conversion rate itself. Go back to your Referral Book and ask yourself if there is anything more you can do to help your champions understand how to set up the introduction better. Personally, I would prefer to wait an extra couple of weeks for a referral if I know that the person referring me has had a more detailed conversation and the person being referred has a genuine interest in what I have to offer, rather than a general curiosity.

Could your requests be more targeted? In other words, if you're being too general in what you ask for, are you getting referred to too many of the wrong people who don't really need your help, or simply aren't in the market for what you offer at the price you offer it?

Is your follow-up effective enough – is it working? Look at how you've followed up those referrals that have turned into business and those that haven't. Is there a distinction between the two? Perhaps it's the time you've taken to get back in touch, whether there's been a telephone conversation before a meeting, even where the meeting has taken place.

When you look at conversion rates, also look at the difference between referrals to people who may introduce you in turn and those direct to prospects. You need to take the referrals to introducers out of the equation, or a better approach would be to work out your conversion rate from referrals offered by such people and credit that back to the original introduction.

As suggested above, you could also group your different referral sources into different channels, such as professional introducers, friends and family, clients and particular industries. It is quite likely that each will offer a different conversion rate, giving you more information on which to base your strategy and work out where your resources and focus are best spent.

REVIEW

This chapter has covered the following:

1 Tracking back new business to its originator to focus your time and effort on proven referral souces.

2 Ensuring a referrals strategy is in place with:
   - fair goals for a realistic return
   - the realisation that patience is a referrals virtue
   - sufficient resources allocated for a referrals strategy
   - a recognition of the patterns of a successful referrals strategy
   - plans for improving your conversion rates
   - determination to nurture your champions on a long-term basis.

In a nutshell
TEN STEPS TO AN EFFECTIVE REFERRALS STRATEGY

You should now have a clear idea of how to put your referrals strategy into place and the tools to help you do so. As an easy reference guide for you, here are 10 quick tips on how to get started.

WHAT ARE YOU LOOKING FOR?

TIP ONE – UNDERSTAND THE DIFFERENCE BETWEEN A TIP, LEAD, RECOMMENDATION AND REFERRAL

There are many different types of business information we can receive. There is a greater chance that the introduction will convert into business if the quality of the interaction between our 'champion' and our prospect is strong.

A tip is a piece of information that indicates someone needs our product or service; a lead will give us a contact name and number. In both cases there is still a lot of work to do and they are just the start of the sales process. At this stage our prospect knows nothing about us – we have just been told about them.

People often mistake recommendations for referrals. If I tell someone about your services and suggest that you can help them, I am recommending you. I'd then pass your number to your prospect and suggest they call. If they do ring, that's great. You will convert more of this type of inquiry than any other. After all, the prospect is already motivated enough to pick up the phone and place a call to you. However, how many opportunities do you miss because your champions have recommended you to people who don't pick up the phone and so you never knew they existed?

So, tips and leads leave us with a lot of work to do. Recommendations leave us looking at the phone and waiting for it to ring. Referrals, however, make life so much easier.

There are three steps to referral heaven:

1 Someone has a need you can fulfil, a problem you can solve or a desire you can satisfy.

2 Your champion recognises this need and speaks to the prospect. Following that conversation, they are interested in how you can help.

3 They are expecting your call.

TIP TWO – WHO IS YOUR IDEAL REFERRAL?

Ask many businesspeople this question and they will struggle to answer. If they can, they will describe a typical client. Let's imagine for a moment that you need 100 clients in a year to meet your targets and you convert one in every three referrals into business. Therefore, you are looking for 300 'ideal referrals' every year. Does that sound achievable to you?

If, like most people, you feel that sounds unrealistic, you're probably right. Getting to that level through a referrals strategy is, however, not such a huge task, if you take the right steps.

Take some time to work out the most powerful introductions you could receive. They could be to clients with whom there is the opportunity to provide a range of services over a long period of time. They could be to people who speak to many of your potential clients and can introduce you on an ongoing basis. They may even be to someone like a newspaper editor who can provide you with good publicity that will help you reach thousands of prospects.

If someone asks 'How can I help you?', don't waste the opportunity by not knowing how best to respond. Do your homework first and understand the introductions that will have the biggest impact on your business.

WHERE WILL THEY COME FROM?

TIP THREE – RECOGNISE WHO'S IN YOUR NETWORK

Think 'referral' and most people think of their clients. That's a natural link – after all, our clients are the people who know the value of what we deliver best, so shouldn't they be the people to refer us? They are. But they are not the only ones.

Other people look to networking events for referrals. You can meet people at networking events who may refer you, but you will still have to build a relationship first, inviting them into your network. It is from your network that you get the support and referrals you need. Events are just a way to build your network and make it stronger.

> it is from your network that you get the support and referrals you need

You are surrounded by people who might be in a fantastic position to refer you, but you may not have recognised that. Look back at your list of ideal referrals. Now think about the people in your network and who they know. Think of your friends, family, suppliers and old colleagues. Think about people you meet socially or parents of children who go to school with yours.

We pigeonhole people based on our relationship with them and interact accordingly. Everyone in your network has a network of their own, however. If your relationship is strong they will probably be happy to help you – you just have to recognise how.

IN A NUTSHELL

TIP FOUR – KNOW WHO TO TURN TO FOR REFERRALS

To decide who is best placed to refer you, look at three key factors:

1 How much do they trust you and your business? Will they want to refer and help you? Will they go out of their way to look for opportunities? And how persuasive and committed will they be when speaking to your prospects?

2 How well do they understand what you do? Can they recognise opportunities for you without your prospects spelling it out? In other words, can they tell from someone's situation that they will have a problem that you can resolve? When speaking to your prospect, do they have a strong enough understanding to answer initial questions and arouse sufficient interest for the prospect to want you to call?

3 Opportunity to refer. Do they speak to the right people? Are they influential in the right circles? After all, your mother may trust you and understand what you do, but is she in a position to be able to refer you?

TIP FIVE – PICK FIVE POTENTIAL CHAMPIONS

Now that you have a clearer picture of who is in your network and who is best placed to refer you, write down five names of people you think could be referring you but either aren't at the moment or could do so more. Don't restrict yourself to the obvious candidates – challenge yourself. Who haven't you thought of as potential referrers before who would fulfil the three criteria above? If you asked them to refer you, how would they feel about it? Try to sense their gut reaction.

don't restrict yourself to the obvious candidates – challenge yourself

Give each of the five a score out of 10 for the three criteria above. How do you think they would rate on each scale? Is that where you want them to be to refer you?

HELPING PEOPLE REFER YOU

TIP SIX – PUT YOURSELF IN THEIR SHOES

Do you get frustrated that you have built a network but don't get the right quality referrals?

When you communicate with your champions, you may make a lot of assumptions about how well they understand your business and how easily they can recognise someone in need of your help. You may be surrounded by people who'd love to refer you but have no idea how or who to.

When someone refers you, a conversation takes place that you are not part of. To ensure that enough of the right conversations take place, you need to put yourself in the shoes of your champions. What do they need to know to:

→ recognise the right opportunities for you?

→ feel comfortable opening the conversation and suggesting your solution?

→ make the other person interested enough to expect your call?

Once you understand how to equip people to refer you effectively, you can be more specific in the way you communicate that information to them.

TIP SEVEN – MAKE IT PERSONAL TO THEM

Many businesses take a general approach to requesting referrals. They will make a broad request to as many people as possible, often along the lines of, 'If you know anyone else who might benefit from our services …'

This is a less than effective approach. Most people won't bother; you haven't been specific enough in your request to make it easy for them. Too broad a request will leave them needing to think about who they know who fits the bill. And many simply won't do the work involved.

Instead, do the filtering for them, asking them for a specific connection they recognise easily. Look at each champion individually and ask yourself, 'Who do they know?' If you understand their network and what is easy for them to understand, you can then ask for the right connections – ones that they are comfortable making.

TIP EIGHT – GET YOUR MESSAGE RIGHT

The more specific the request, the easier it becomes to make it clear to people why the referral is so relevant. On the whole, people are motivated either by desires or by needs. Communicate clearly to your champions the desires you satisfy or needs you meet and how that makes a difference to your clients. They will then find the ensuing conversation with your prospect so much easier.

Assuming that you are with the majority of business-to-business service providers, if your business solves problems for your clients, there is a very simple structure to the message you need to share with your champions. Once you have identified who you would like them to introduce you to:

→ explain what problem they are likely to be facing;

→ outline the solution you provide;

→ make it clear how your clients then benefit as a result.

Use this model as a spine for case studies that illustrate how you have helped people in a similar position previously, but keep it simple and stick to this structure.

FOLLOWING UP

TIP NINE – TRACK THE RESULTS

Word of mouth marketing and referrals should be as close to the core of any business strategy as other lead-generation and business development tools. If you don't track and measure your activity, how can you possibly know what works, what you should shed and how to improve your return?

Use the Referral Book system to help prompt referral activity, monitor what comes in and track the results. It will allow you to work out how best to inspire different groups to refer them, ensure promises of referrals are followed up and measure what business comes in through referral.

A focused approach such as this also ensures that there is more focus on generating new referrals. Rather than leaving recommendation and referral to chance, the business can actively seek them, leading naturally to a much higher return.

TIP TEN – SAY 'THANK YOU'

Such an obvious note on which to finish. I was amazed at the number of people who approached me after one talk I gave on referrals to tell me how they had forgotten to thank people for referring them.

If you don't thank people, pretty soon they will feel taken for granted and stop referring you. Make them feel good and feel appreciated. If you make the experience of referring you a positive one, they will be more likely to do so again.

> make them feel good and feel appreciated

Even if a referral isn't right or doesn't come off, thank people. Let them know what has happened or why the fit isn't right, but show that you appreciate the support. Pass it on to someone better suited to follow it up if appropriate, but let your champion know and make sure they are comfortable with you doing so.

Don't just thank people the once. Keep them in the loop as the referral develops and, of course, thank them again when it matures into business.

Further resources

NETWORKING AND SALES BLOGS

The Networking Blog – Keep up to date with my regular thoughts and advice on networking – **www.lopata.co.uk/blog**

The National Networker – The US-based weekly publication for which I write a monthly column – **www.thenationalnetworker.com**

Business Networking – Blog from US founder of BNI and best-selling author Ivan Misner – **www.businessnetworking.com**

Bob Burg – Regular ideas on referrals from one of the masters – **www.burg.com/blog/**

Brian Tracy – A wide range of support from one of the world's leading business and self-development experts – **www.briantracy.com/blog/**

Business Networking Blog – Short and snappy networking tips and podcasts from CEO of UK-based NRG Networks, Dave Clarke – **www.nrg-networks.com/nrg-networking-blog.html**

The Networking Coach's Opinion – Blog from Belgian author of *Let's Connect* and *How to Really Use LinkedIn*, Jan Vermeiren – **www.janvermeiren.com**

Networking Insight – Straightforward and simple networking advice from Chicago's Jason Jacobsohn – **www.networkinginsight.com**

Social Media Marketing and Business Promotion – Blog from Warren Cass including a host of excellent guest bloggers – **www.warrencass.com**

Just Professionals – Great blogs on how to use social media for business development from UK architect Su Butcher – **www.justprofessionals.net**

Business Scene – Your guide to finding networks around the UK, together with some pretty good events they run themselves – **www.business-scene.com**

Joined Up Business Networking – Networking tips from Heather Townsend, author of *The FT Guide to Business Networking* – **joinedupnetworking.com**

Find Networking Events – UK-wide directory of networking events, split by region; also has regional section for women's events – **www.findnetworkingevents.com**

BUSINESS NETWORKS

The Professional Speaking Association – For anyone who speaks for a living – **www.professionalspeaking.biz/**

NRG Networks – Monthly meetings in various UK locations – **www.nrg-networks.com**

Academy for Chief Executives – Peer-to-peer mastermind groups for CEOs, senior directors and entrepreneurs – **www.chiefexecutive.com**

Vistage – Peer mastermind groups for senior executives – **www.vistage.com**

BNI – Weekly referral-focused business networking meetings – **www.bni.com**

BRX – My old company; referral-focused networking – **www.brxnet.co.uk**

4Networking – An online community and regular breakfast meetings, without the level of commitment of BNI or BRX – **www.4networking.biz**

Business 4 Breakfast – Regular referral-focused breakfast meetings – **http://www.bforb.com**

European Professional Women's Network – A network focused on the development of professional women; very proactive with a range of events – **www.europeanpwn.net**

Women in Technology – Career opportunities and excellent events for women in IT industries – **www.womenintechnology.co.uk**

Women in Banking and Finance – Professional organisation committed to empowering its members in the banking and finance industry – **www.wibf.org.uk**

Sister Snog – Women's networking with attitude – **sistersnog.socialgo.com**

1230 The Women's Company – Local women's network for both support and referrals – **www.1230.co.uk**

The Athena Network – For women in a business development role – **www.theathenanetwork.com**

International Special Events Society – Excellent network if you are in the events industry; chapters worldwide – **www.ises.com**

London Launch – For the events industry and meeting planners in London – **www.londonlaunch.com**

LinkedIn – The online platform for generating business referrals – **www.linkedin.com**

Twitter – Great for spreading your message quickly and virally – **www.twitter.com**

Facebook – Mainly for friends and family but increasingly used for business – **www.facebook.com**

Ecademy.com – Online networking, predominantly for profile building among smaller businesses; very strong in the UK – **www.ecademy.com**

Xing.com – Good business network with strong membership on the European continent – **www.xing.com**

FURTHER READING

Matt Anderson (2009), *Fearless Referrals*. Booksurge.

Andy Bounds (2007), *The Jelly Effect*. Capstone.

Bob Burg (1998), *Endless Referrals*. McGraw-Hill.

Graham Codrington and Sue Grant-Marshall (2004), *Mind the Gap!* The Penguin Group.

Graham Davies (2011), *The Presentation Coach. Base Knuckle Brillance for Every Presenter*. Capstone.

Steven D'Souza (2010), *Brilliant Networking*. Prentice Hall.

Lesley Everett (2004), *Walking Tall*. Lesley Everett.

Keith Ferrazzi (2011), *Never Eat Alone*. Doubleday.

Mindy Gibbins Klein (2009), *24 Carat Bold*. Ecademy Press.

Jeffrey Gitomer (2006), *Little Black Book of Connections*. Bard Press.

Andy Gooday (2009), *Get Well Connected*. Fresh Future Ltd.

Vanessa Hall (2009), *The Truth about Trust in Business*. Emerald Book Co.

Carol Harris (2000), *Networking for Success*. Oak Tree Press.

Barrie Hopson and Katie Ledger (2009), *And What Do You Do?* A & C Black Publishers Ltd.

Bruce King (2010), *How to Double your Sales*. Financial Times Prentice Hall.

Grant Leboff (2007), *Sales Therapy*. Capstone Publishing.

Grant Leboff (2011), *Sticky Marketing*. Kogan Page.

Andy Lopata and Peter Roper (2011), *... and Death Came Third! The Definitive Guide to Networking and Speaking in Public*. Second edition. Ecademy Press.

Andy Lopata, Stephen Harvard Davis and Terence P. O'Halloran (2005), *Building a Business on Bacon and Eggs*. Life Publications Ltd.

Leil Lowndes (2008), *How to Talk to Anyone*. Thorsons.

Angela Marshall (2008), *Being Truly You*. Matador.

Abraham Maslow (1943), 'A theory of human motivation', *Psychological Review* 50(4), 370–96.

Ivan Misner and Don Morgan (2000), *Masters of Networking*. Bard Press.

Linda Parkinson-Hardman (2010), *LinkedIn Made Easy*. Lulu.com.

Susan RoAne (2000), *How to Work a Room*. HarperCollins.

Roy Sheppard (2001), *Rapid Result Referrals*. Centre Publishing.

James Surowiecki (2005), *The Wisdom of Crowds*. Abacus.

Heather Townsend (2011), *The Financial Times Guide to Business Networking*. FT Prentice Hall.

Jan Vermieren (2007), *Let's Connect*. Morgan James Publishing.

Jan Vermieren (2009), *How to REALLY Use LinkedIn*. Booksurge Publishing.

Richard White (2011), *Networking Survival Guide*. Lean Marketing Press.

Index

Page numbers in *italics* denotes a figure/table

Ablestoke Consulting and HR
   108–10
Academy for Chief Executives 34
acquaintances (weak ties) 124–5
advertising 52–4
affiliate schemes 186, 187
Amazon xx
appearance
   and trust 65
Arndt, Mikael 97, 98
asking for referrals 35–6, 76,
      199–204
   common approaches 31, 201,
      215
   and LinkedIn 233–6, *235*
   and one-to-one meetings
      203–4
   right timing 23, 202–4
   wrong timing 30–2, 200–2

Baum, David 25
Beecham, Sinclair 184–5
Bibesco, Elizabeth 195
blogging 160
Bond, Tim 229
brain building
   and networks 157–8
   and social networks 160
Bribery Act (2010) 192
Brown, John Seely 208
Buist, William 71
Burnage, Mike 34
business associations 125

business cards 8–9
Business Network International
      (BNI) 158
Business Referral Exchange
      (BRX) 6
business relationships
   mixing with personal
      relationships 136–8
Business Scene 71
buying decisions
   influences on 58, *59, 60*

Carnegie, Dale
   *How to Win Friends and
      Influence People* 190–1
case studies 96, 97–8, 244, 264
Cass, Warren 71
Chambers of Commerce 19, 125
champions 123
   being specific about requests
      to 92–3, 94, 242–3, 256,
      263–4
   bringing back into the fold
      253–4
   competitors as 106–7
   feedback to 194–5, 245–6
   identifying potential 75–6,
      102–5, 240–2, *240*, 262
   making them understand your
      message and who you
      want to meet 80–7, 90–1,
      94–6, 241, 244
   painting pictures of who you
      would like to meet 94–6

champions (*continued*)
> putting yourself in their shoes
>> 75–6, 80, 263
>
> recognising the opportunity to
>> refer you 88–90, 242
>
> standing out from the crowd
>> when looking for 103–4
>
> thanking 265–6
>
> tracking your interactions with
>> 250
>
> understanding of their network
>> and conversations they
>> are having 89–90, 197,
>> 241–2
>
> willingness to refer 74–5, 241
>
> winning referrals from 242–4

'chemistry' 126

Cialdini, Robert
> *Influence: The Psychology of*
>> *Persuasion* 201

Clarke, David 174–5

clients
> network of *135*
>
> and referrals xx, 28, 30, 35, 132,
>> 261

cold-calling 11–12, 13, 25, 45–8,
> 251–2
>
> tips for better 47

commissions 186–7

common interests, establishing of
> 68–9, 126

competitors
> and referrals 106–10

conversion rates 255–7

corporate entertainment 192–3

Covey , Stephen
> *The Seven Habits of Highly*
>> *Effective People* 210

cross-referring 107–10, 147–51

cross-selling charts 149

customer review sites xx, xxi

Davies, Martine 134

Davison, Lang 208

digital media
> extending your networks
>> through 116–17
>
> *see also* social networks/
>> networking

direct mail 38–9, 48–50

Direct Mail Association
> Response Rate Trend Report
>> (2010) 38

direct response marketing 38–9,
> 48–50

door-to-door sales operations 45,
> 201

Ecademy 119, 160, 161
> BlackStar level of 71, 161

elevator pitches 16, 20, 21, 22,
> 70, 95

emails
> Magic 235–6
>
> and making introductions 10,
>> 216–17
>
> marketing 39, 48–9

empathetic listening 210

empathy 69–70, 209

employees, former
> as source of referrals 134

endorsements *see* testimonials

entertainment
> using of to inspire referrals
>> 192–4

Everett, Lesley 66, 84–5

expectations
> exceeding of and referrals
>> 33–4, *33*
>
> and trust 66–7, 68

experience
> building trust up through 71–3

Facebook 53, 117, 119, 160

Faith, Natasha 128

family/friends
> mixing business with 137, 142
>
> as part of your network 16, 88,
>> *123*, 132, *132*, 261

as potential referral sources
138, 240
feedback 84
to your champion 194–5, 245–6
51-51 equation 190–2
financial incentives *see* incentives
first impressions 65–6
focus, retaining 196–7
forecasting 252–3
former employees
as source of referrals 134

gatekeepers 11–12
Givers Gain 172–3, 195, 196, 206
giving referrals 181–4, 189, 205–18
exercise 181–3, *182, 183,* 206
and Givers Gain 172–3, 195,
196, 206
introductions 214–15, 216–18
and listening 210–11, 215
making the right connection
215–16
safeguarding your reputation
212–13
showing a real interest in others
207
and tacit knowledge 208–9
time and effort factor 213–14,
213
timing 211–12
giving/receiving balance 195–6
Gladwell, Malcolm
The Tipping Point 117–18
Google AdWords 53
Google Alerts 72
Granovetter , Mark
The Strength of Weak Ties
124–5
Guare, John 116

Hagel III, John 208
Hall, Vanessa 66
Heath, Chip and Dan
Made to Stick 96
'Holy Quadruplicate' 103

'How can I help you?' question
80–3, 200, 212, 261

ideal referral, identifying 42–4, *43,*
81, 87, 260–1
incentive schemes 40–1, 184, 185
industry associations 157
interests, establishing common
68–9, 126
introducer fees 185–6
introducers *see* champions
introductions 4
and emails 10, 216–17
and giving referrals 214–15,
216–18
and meetings 217–18

jargon 95–6

Karinthy, Frigyes 114

lapsed referrals 253–4
lead-generation 29, 31, 201, 215
leads 7–8, 9, 259, 260
Leboff, Grant
Sticky Marketing xix
LinkedIn xvii, 72, 117, 140, 160,
204, 221–37
asking for a referral 233–6, *235*
building your network 227–9
and endorsements/testimonials
72, 230–1, *230*
profile 224–6, *226*
current and past positions
226
message 225
photograph 224
professional experience and
goals 225, *226*
specialities 226
status 225, *225*
and referral building 160–1,
231–3, *232*
and six degrees of separation
222

LinkedIn Open Networkers 119
listen to/listen for 210
listening, art of 210–11, 215
Lopata, Andy
 ...and Death Came Third 126,
  210
losing work 194
loyalty schemes 184–5

McKinsey 138
Magic Email 235–6
mailshots 38, 48–50
marketing 45–54
 advertising 52–4
 cold-calling see cold-calling
 direct response 38–9, 48–50
 email 39, 48–9
 perils of mass 38–40, 42, 44
 and public relations 51–2
Marshall, Angela 65
Maslow's Hierarchy of Needs 67
mass marketing, perils of 38–40,
  42, 44
meetings
 and introductions 217–18
 see also one-to-one meetings
message
 and case studies 97–8
 getting it right 264
 and Problem-Solution-Benefit
  model 94–6
 and referral mix 169–71
 refining of 250
 understanding and conveying of
  to your champion
  80–7, 90–1, 94–6, 241, 244
 using simple language and not
  jargon 95–6
Milgram, Professor Stanley 115,
  117, 118
Misner, Ivan 117, 118, 172, 173,
  195
 Truth or Delusion 119–20

Mouazan, Servane 190
multi-level marketing (MLM)
  companies 29
Mutton, Neil 109–10

names and numbers approach 6,
  29, 30–1, 215
National Speakers' Association
  106
Nead, Howard 53
needs 104
 focusing on prospect's 46
 and trust 67
networking dance 20–1
networking events 16, 261
 building up of relationships at
  17, 18–19, 20, 21–2, 23
 and going for the immediate
  return 23
 not focusing on selling 141–2
 within organisations 149
networking groups 125, 154–5
 classification of 155–9
 developing friendships within
  18
 distinction between networks
  and 17–18
 getting results from your
  membership 163–4
 importance of in building up
  networks 126
 leaving 173–5
 limitations 19, 154–5
 networking myth and referrals
  17–19, 154
 selecting the right one for you
  154
 setting clear goals 163, 164
 visitor days 154
 and 'who do you know who'
  question 91
networking myth 17–19, 154
networking overload 25

NetworkingSunday.com 229
networks/networking 16, 17–18
    and 51-51 equation 190–2
    and brain building 157–8
    building up deep relationships
            within your 17, 24, 123,
            126–7, 190–2
    building of within organisations
            149
    classification of 155–9
    and commitment 171–2
    defining and types of 16
    degrees of your 123–4, *123*
    distinction between networking
            groups and 17–18
    forecasting return on investment
            from 252–3
    Givers Gain concept 172–3
    hidden connections of people in
            your 88–90, 132–5, 211
    long-term approach 127–9, 251
    making manageable 122–3
    making real connections
            through conversation
            121–4
    mixing business and personal
            136–8
    need for diversity 119–20, 125
    online 159–62
        see *also* social networks/
            networking
    pigeonholing people in your
            132–3, *132*, 210, 261
    power of weak ties 124–5
    and profile building 155–7
    and referral building 158–9
    and referrals mix 166–9
    returns from xxi, 163–7, 252–3
    selecting the right one for you
            153–75
    selling through and not to
            140–2
    setting objectives from 162, *162*
    and six degrees of separation
            117–18, 119
    size of 119–21, 122
    socialising with people in your
            70–1
    tracking the connections you
            need 139–40
    ways of building up a positive
            profile among fellow
            members 172
    ways of growing your 125–7
niche markets, establishing 105
Nielsen Global Online Consumer
        Survey 58
non-specific requests 39–40, 42,
        44, 92–3, 263–4

one-to-one meetings 70, 172, 190,
        203–4
online advertising 53
online networking 159–62
    see *also* social networks/
            networking
organisations
    building your internal network
            within 149
    internal networking events 149
    lack of inter-departmental
            communication 146–7
    mixing of staff within 149
    personal targets and rewards
            150–1
    referral partnership between
            107–9
    referrals within 145–51
    trust and understanding within
            147–9

passive referrals approach 32–3,
        180, 181, 185
'pay per click' 53
personal brand 66, 84–5

personal lives,
    keeping separate from business
        lives 136–8
Plaxo 229
positive referral cycle 76–7, *76*
Precious Online Awards 128
press, tips in dealing with 52
Preston, Andy 47
Pret à Manger 184, 185
Priestley , Daniel 186
proactive, being 35–6, 77, 107,
        180, 222, 253
Problem-Solution-Benefit model
        94–6, 97–8
Professional Speaking Association
        157
profile building
    and networks 155–7
    and social networks 160
promises, and trust 67–8
prospects xv, 9, 30, 87–8
    developing a picture of 139
    eliciting response from 97–8
    knowing about you in advance
        and expecting telephone
        call 9, 10
public relations 51–2

Q&A People Matter 108–10
qualified referrals 62–3, 75, 212
questions, asking the right 91–3
Quin~essence 109–10

rapport 68
receiving/giving balance 195–6
reciprocity 173, 200
recommendations 8–9, 259–60
referral-aware 28, 30
Referral Book xxii, 239–47, 254,
        255, 265
    identifying potential champions
        240–2, *240*
    as a tool 246–7

tracking referrals 244–6, *245*
winning referrals 242–4
referral heaven, three steps to
        9–11, 260
Referral Institute 204
referral mix 166–71, *168*
referral partnership between firms
        107–9
referrals
    asking for *see* asking for
        referrals
    and being proactive 35–6, 77,
        107, 180, 222, 253
    benefits of xix, xx, 4, 12–13
    and exceeding expectations
        33–4, *33*
    giving *see* giving referrals
    identifying ideal 42–4, *43*, 81,
        87, 260–1
    inspiring people to make
        179–204
    keeping in touch after passing
        on 73
    key foundations for success
        158, 216
    lapsed 253–4
    main barrier to regular 180
    as the most effective route to
        market 44–5
    passive approach 32–3, 180,
        181, 185
    people's preference for 4–5
    qualified 62–3, 75, 212
    relational approaches 184,
        188–9
    shift from quantity to quality of 6
    tracking 244–6, 250–2, 254, 265
    transactional approaches
        184–8
    unqualified 63–4, 75
    ways to make it worthwhile for
        people to refer you 194–5

winning 242–4
within an organisation 145–51
referrals strategy 28–9
long-term approach 251
ten steps to an effective
259–66
trust and understanding as key
foundations for 30, 147,
159
rejection-then-retreat technique
201
relational approaches 184, 188–9
relationships 197–8, 208
and 51-51 equation 190–2
avoiding networking overload
25–6
between different parts of an
organisation 147–9
building of at networking events
17, 18–19, 20, 21–2, 23
building deep 17, 24, 123,
126–7, 190–2
developing of outside the
networking event 70–1,
172, 190
and sharing common interests
68–9, 126
ways to stay in touch with other
people 192
reputation
safeguarding of when giving
referrals 212–13
requests
non-specific 39–40, 42, 44,
92–3, 263–4
specific 92–3, 94, 242–3, 256,
263–4
returns
from networks xxi, 163–7, 252–3
Robert, Cavett 106
Rotary 125
Rothenberg, Randall 53
Round Table 125

selling
avoiding of in networking 140–2
Six Degrees Game 117–18
six degrees of separation 114–19,
123, 132, 139, 166
social networks/networking 53,
159–62, 222
brain building 160
profile building 160
referral building 160–2
testimonials on 72–3
see also LinkedIn
specific requests, making 92–3,
94, 242–3, 256, 263–4
speed networking 80–1, 200
staff canteen 149
standing out from the crowd 103–4
Stevens, Alan 51–2, 160
Stevenson, Aron 193
story-telling 94–5, 97–8
successes, replicating existing
254–5
Sunday Times Wine Club 40, 184
synergy groups, setting up of
107–9

tacit knowledge 208–9
targets 150–1
Tel Aviv University 32
testimonials 72
and LinkedIn 72, 230–1, 230
and online social networks 72–3
thank you, saying 265–6
Thomson, Peter 49–50
time and effort factor
and giving referrals 213–14, 213
timing
and asking for referrals 23,
30–2, 200–4
and giving referrals 211–12
tips 7, 9, 259, 260
tracking referrals 244–6, 250–2,
254, 265

transactional approaches 184–8

trigger comments 214

TripAdvisor xx

trust 58, 76–7, 193–4, 209, 243
    building up of through
        experience 71–3
    building up of through one-to-
        one meetings 70
    definition 66
    developing relationships outside
        the networking event and
        70–1
    establishing 64–5
    establishing common interests
        and 68–9
    factors influencing 64–5
    and first impressions 65–6
    fulfilling promises 67–8
    as key foundation for referral
        strategy xxi, 30, 58, 76–7,
        76
    understanding expectations and
        needs 66–7, 68
    within organisations 147–9

Twitter 119, 160, 161

'underpromise and overdeliver' 34

unqualified referrals 63–4, 75

unsolicited sales calls 12

values, core 66

Vermeiren, Jan 235–6

visitor days 154

Wax, Ruby 69–70

weak ties, strength of 124–5

weather, talking about the 68–70

Westwood, Tony 169–71

who do you refer exercise 181–4,
    182, 183

'Wild Card Pack, The' 127–8

willingness to refer 74–5, 241

women's networks 149

word of mouth marketing xx–xxi, 5

Xing 160

Zemikael, Semhal 128

Ziegler, James A. 65

JOIN THE CONVERSATION

Having reached the end of this book, I hope you have already taken your first steps towards developing an effective referrals strategy. There may be questions you want answered or tips you'd like to share with other people going through the same process.

Please join the conversation on Twitter, Facebook or LinkedIn.

- On **Twitter** you can ask me a question or share your experiences at **@AndyLopata** or use the tag **#RecommendedtheBook**.

- On **Facebook** please sign up for my Connecting is not Enough page at **www.facebook.com/networkingstrategy** where I will share blogs and ideas relevant to networking strategies, and encourage you to do the same and also answer questions.

- On **LinkedIn** you can join the Business Networking Strategy group (search for 'Business Networking Strategy' under groups) where you can also ask questions and join in general discussions.

For further information on how I can support you to implement a referrals strategy in your business, and for more resources to support your networking, please visit **www.lopata.co.uk** or send me an email at **andy@lopata.co.uk**.

I also send out a three-weekly networking tips e-zine and you can subscribe to this at **www.lopata.co.uk**.

Last, but not least, if you have found this book to be valuable, please help me by recommending it to your network. If you are an Amazon customer, could you also please post a review on the site and share what made a difference to you?

Happy networking!

Andy Lopata

Read On

9780273745518

9780273742326

9780273750444

9780273732617

Available online and from all good bookstores

...and death came third!

- *Do you dread going to networking events?*
- *Do you hide at the back of the room when you have the opportunity to present your business?*

In 1984 a New York Times Survey on Social Anxiety placed death third in the list of people's biggest fears. The top two responses were walking into a room full of strangers and speaking in public.

Facing these two fears head on, '...and death came third!' rocketed straight to Number Two on the Amazon UK bestseller lists on publication of its First Edition in 2006. Since then thousands of people have turned to its pages to help them network and present with much more confidence.

In this updated second edition you can discover how to:

- Walk into a networking event and approach people with CONFIDENCE
- STRUCTURE a talk so that you can get your key message across POWERFULLY
- ENGAGE people in conversation and get them interested in YOU
- FOCUS on the results you want from networking and achieve them EASILY
- STAND and speak with CONVICTION and AUTHORITY

and much, much more...

Brought to you by:

Andy Lopata,
Business Networking
Strategist.

Peter Roper,
The Natural
Presenter.

ISBN: 9781907722301
Format: Paperback B&W
Size: 216 x 140 mm
Page Count: 280 pp
Price: £15.99

www.anddeathcamethird.com
Available from Amazon and all good bookstores.